Directed by Jack Arnold

Directed by
Jack Arnold

by
Dana M. Reemes

with a Foreword by
FORREST J ACKERMAN

McFarland & Company, Inc., Publishers
Jefferson, North Carolina, and London

Frontispiece: Jack Arnold in the late 1960s, on location in Italy for the television series *It Takes a Thief.*

Library of Congress Cataloguing-in-Publication Data

Reemes, Dana M.
Directed by Jack Arnold.

Bibliography: p. 235.
Filmography: p. 213.
Includes index.
1. Arnold, Jack, 1912–   —Criticism and
interpretation.   I. Title.
PN1998.3.A76R44   1988   791.43′0233′0924   87-46382

ISBN 0-89950-331-4 (50# acid-free natural paper)

Printed in the United States of America.

McFarland & Company, Inc., Publishers
Box 611, Jefferson, North Carolina 28640

To my parents

Table of Contents

Forryword

(In which Forrest J Ackerman reminisces about Jack Arnold, "The Incredible Thinking Man.")

His directorial style has been called clean . . . spare . . . down to Earth (even when out of this world).

In a word: Direct.

There is a lengthy saga concerning how I managed (aided and abetted by William Nolan of *Logan's Run* fame) to outfox the would-be studio frustrators and sneak in on the sneak preview of *It Came from Outer Space*. Nolan, Ray Harryhausen (wizard of stop-motion animation) and I were forced to strain our necks, sitting in the front row of the theater, but it was worth it to be present in the first audience viewing of the cinemadaptation of Bradbury's screen treatment of "The Meteor." The wizard of words was pleased with the result of the metamorphosis—"85 percent of what I wrote reached the screen," he said—and we viewers were pleased with what the director had thoughtfully translated to the screen.

I didn't realize it at the time but this was the *firstime* I was seeing the fine Martian hand of one Jack Arnold.

In fact, the one and only Jack Arnold.

The year of his imagi-movie debut was 1953—the year of the first Hugo awards—and the film was in 3-D, a process which I have been given to understand Jack Arnold helped develop.

The following year, out of the murky depths of Universal's back lot lake (and once again in a three-dimensional process), there emerged *The Creature from the Black Lagoon*, a favorite among fantasy film fans.

ix

Jack's *Tarantula!* was no *Fly* or *Black Scorpion*, but Arnold extracted what he could from a mediocre script, improving it with the Arnold directorial touch.

Then came the fortuitous combination of Arnold and scriptwriter Richard Matheson and an imaginative masterpiece was born: *The Incredible Shrinking Man.* Arnold's direction was dexterous as he created an instant, enduring scientific classic. A projected sequel, *The Incredible Little Girl,* very likely would have been to the original as *The Bride of Frankenstein* was to *Frankenstein* and would have been another fondly remembered Arnold film, but the script, alas, was not produced as a followup. He had nothing to do with the miserable farce that was perpetrated many years later.

Arnold's final excursion into the realm of fantastic cinema was the whimsical Leonard Wibberly work *The Mouse That Roared* in 1959.

In 1984 he was preparing a remake of the Sir Arthur Conan Doyle enduring 1925 silent classic *The Lost World,* but plans for its production were abandoned, leaving it in the Realm of Unwrought Things.

Pity!

Forrest J Ackerman
Hollywood, 1987

Preface

Jack Arnold, distinguished genre and science-fiction director, and 3-D pioneer, has become recognized in recent years as an artist of international repute. The many articles and occasional book chapters that have appeared both here and abroad attest to this, as do the retrospectives and frequent revivals of some of his most remarkable films. Despite this growing interest, no complete feature filmography of Arnold's work has yet appeared, much less an overview of his entire career. The following pages are offered as a first attempt at placing his best-loved films in the larger context of his work as a whole, all set against the historical background in which the films were made. This treatment not only provides further evidence of Arnold's virtuoso mastery of the popular film, but also draws attention to some of his lesser-known pictures. In addition, an attempt has been made to document the director's methods and his attitude toward the medium.

It is primarily through the generosity of Mr. Arnold and his wife Betty that this study was at all possible. Among others deserving my heartfelt thanks are David Shepard of the Director's Guild of America, Doris Plough and Arthur Nadel of Filmation Studios, the staff of the library of the Academy of Motion Picture Arts and Sciences, Randolph Pitts for his many helpful suggestions, and the great Forrest J Ackerman for his invaluable encouragement and support.

Introduction

Art is born of constraint and dies of freedom.
—André Gide

Since the beginning of his feature film career, Jack Arnold has worked almost entirely within the Hollywood system. His most active years were as a studio contract director making mostly program pictures in nearly every genre. Arnold did not often have much choice over the material that he was assigned to direct; the studio was in business to turn out a product and Arnold was essentially an employee. Yet, as we shall see, Arnold's attraction to the medium was due as much to artistic as to pecuniary reasons. Moreover, it was within these very limitations that he directed some of his best and most innovative work, films that have stood the test of time in terms of continued popularity. To Jack Arnold, a dramatic artist in love with the motion picture, being a contract director was not so much a question of limitations as it was of opportunities for creative expression.

In the 1950s, it was the custom at major studios for the talent to sign seven-year contracts. Typically there might be a thousand-dollar raise every year or two, and a provision for yearly options, i.e., the studio could drop you after any given year. As a director, one was given scripts, and was obliged to do any film the studio wanted. If a script was particularly disliked by a director, he might ask for another, and might get another if one was ready to hand. But if one wasn't, a stubborn director might be suspended without pay until he accepted an assignment of the studio's choice. One made the pictures one didn't want to make in order to make the pictures one wanted to.

Lack of choice in subject matter was by no means the end of the

1

limitations imposed on a studio contract director. Budget and time restrictions were very tight, a constant test of one's ingenuity. Some shooting schedules demanded up to eight or ten pages of script a day. To aggravate matters, Universal had a policy (which persists to this day) whereby the assistant director is charged with the responsibility of monitoring a director's daily progress. If the day's shooting seems to be falling behind, the assistant director calls the front office and the production manager comes down to the set to speed things up, hardly ideal conditions for the creation of art. It seems miraculous that films of quality were ever made under such circumstances.

The "B" or program picture had become an established part of the movie business in the mid-1930s when large studio-owned theatre chains made the double-bill their standard format. Generally, the "B" picture was a second feature, filling out a program in which an "A" picture was the principal attraction, though sometimes, especially in neighborhood theatres—the "matineé" trade—the program might consist of two "B" pictures in addition to the customary shorts, cartoons, newsreels, and trailers. In some rural areas where the single feature format lingered on, the feature attraction was often a "B" action picture. All the major studios had their "B" units, while a number of smaller "B" studios also came into being. The number of these films produced through the late 1940s was truly prodigious. By the time Jack Arnold arrived in Hollywood in 1949, the program picture had passed its peak but continued to be produced in dwindling numbers for another decade or so. Through the 1950s, the major studio "B" was still the testing ground for new talent, and was the natural beginning of Arnold's Hollywood career.

Twenty or thirty years after these films were made, we may choose to regard them less as a commercial product than as part of our cultural heritage. Their sheer popularity and survival validates them. It might even be said that genre program pictures preserve a more vivid and accurate picture of ourselves, our ideas, desires or preoccupations than more deliberately artful, personal, and expensive pictures do. Films once dismissed as low-budget, merely "standard" genre melodramas are now being appreciated as artifacts, aesthetic objects to be judged not on the basis of budgets or commercial success but for their often novel and ingeniously various treatment of standard themes. The modest virtues of the best of these films seem wonderful when compared to the appalling disregard for audience expectation evident in many expensive, arrogant and self-indulgent movies of today. It is true that the "B" movies are "standard," but this can only mean that there were craftsmen working within certain given parameters. Excellence was certainly possible and sometimes attained. There are those people who set the "high standard of standardness," and Jack Arnold is certainly one of them.

The collaborative nature of producing genre pictures is neatly summarized by Stuart Kaminsky:

> The businessman-producer finds a story, or has one written; works with a team of professionals, led by a director; and together they produce a genre film. . . . The writer, director, art director, director of photography, and other contributors to the motion picture play on the elements of the established genre, adding to it their own talents and ideas, often refining details and clarifying the archetype. Clearly, the creative abilities and concerns of the director and his collaborators can make the genre film distinctive and personal at the same time that it serves to retell an old story.[1]

As we shall see in the work of Jack Arnold, the degree of a director's influence may vary considerably from project to project. We cannot lose sight of the limitations within which a director worked.

These very limitations, however, are the key to appreciating a contract director's achievement, for it is the pressures of these limitations that provoke and define a director's artistic response. In Jack Arnold's case this response necessarily varies according to the limits and opportunities presented by each successive project. Beginning his career with a scarcity of resources, he developed a particularly lean, efficient narrative style, typified by extreme deliberation and very low shooting ratio. He developed a very fluid camera, its movements designed for effective narration, but with an eye to "one take" economy. He learned to increase the apparent scope of his pictures with ingenious but inexpensive effects work, and turned his early stage training to good purpose by eliciting fine performances, often from otherwise undistinguished talents. He was sometimes able to have an influence on the content of the stories as well. All this is detailed in the following chapters, which document Arnold's entire career to date, and examine the dynamic tension between the director and his limitations, an aspect of the contest between art and commerce.

1
Getting Started
or
From Stage to Screen

Jack Arnold was born on October 14, 1912, on a kitchen table in New Haven, Connecticut, to young Russian immigrant parents. His maternal grandfather had given them the candy concession at the local Bijou Theatre as a wedding present, and the young family prospered — when they weren't eating up all the profits. In the following years Arnold's sister Sylvia was born and the family moved to New York City, where his father became a successful stockbroker for some years before the crash.

It was naturally hoped that young Jack might aspire to be a doctor or lawyer, but Arnold had a very different ambition — to make a career for himself in theater. His parents did not encourage him in this, and it was younger sister Sylvia who got the piano and tap-dance lessons. Arnold was determined, however, and had Sylvia teach him each dance lesson as she learned it. (Sylvia went on to modest success as a chorine in Broadway shows with stars like Jimmy Durante.) Arnold, meanwhile, began to rehearse comedy routines — mostly crude slapstick and pratfalls — with his best friend, Larry Nadel, whose uncle was a minor vaudeville comedian. Arnold recalls, "We used to enter amateur contests, and were we terrible! I don't think we ever won."

It was about this time that Arnold's father took him for a ride in an open cockpit biplane, awakening an interest in flying that was to be of continued significance for him in later life. He was also an

4

Jack Arnold at six years of age.

eager witness of the great parade celebrating Lindbergh's historic transatlantic crossing.

Within a few brief years came the stock market crash of 1929, and the entire family was living together in a single room. Arnold was now in his late teens, finished with high school, and seriously concerned about his future. Determined as ever to make a career on stage, he set his hopes on being admitted to the American Academy of Dramatic Arts, then in the former little theater under Carnegie

Hall. After a grueling and suspenseful audition he was at last accepted. His classmates included Hume Cronyn, Betty Field, Garsen Kanin, and Martin Gable—all of whom went on to distinguished careers on stage or screen. While still at the Academy, Arnold made his acting debut in a play in New Jersey. Graduating in his early twenties, he went directly to work on Broadway.

Director Maurice Schwartz cast Arnold in the English-language version of *Yoshe Kalb*, the last effort of producer Daniel Frohm, a giant in the theater at the turn of the century who had the peculiar habit of watching performances from a trapdoor in his office above the stage. Arnold then went on to appear in a succession of Broadway hits, working with many of the great luminaries of the golden age of American theater. One of his early breaks was a part in George Abbott's production of *Three Men on a Horse*, in which Arnold eventually replaced star Garsen Kanin when Kanin left to seek his fortune in Hollywood. Arnold's salary was two hundred dollars a week, which was big money in those depression years. In 1936, after a year in New York, Abbott took his production to London for a year; there Arnold worked as stage manager and understudy. He also found time to act in two Edgar Wallace pictures while he was there. Returning to New York, he joined the Kaufman and Hart production *The American Way*, which opened at the then new Rockefeller Center Theater, and continued with Kaufman and Hart in their following play, *The Fabulous Invalid*. He was afterward assistant stage manager for *Dinner at Eight*. He next took a part in Saroyan's *The Time of Your Life*, in which he understudied and later took over from Gene Kelly. In 1940 he produced a musical play, *Bright Lights*, and was assistant producer with Eva LeGallienne for *Alice in Wonderland*.

It was at this time that Arnold began his first experiments in filmmaking. He built a blimp (lined with foam rubber and equipped with external controls) to quiet an old Kodak Model K 16mm camera. When he wasn't working he would go to the theater and discreetly photograph the actors in whatever play they were in at the time. Shooting wide open with fast black-and-white film, Arnold covered a play over a period of three performances; first getting long shots, then going up to the boxes to get angle shots, and returning again with a telephoto lens for close-ups. In this way he obtained enough coverage to edit sequences with perfect continuity. The result was a silent "highlight" reel of a given play. He made up prints and demonstrated them backstage with a portable 16mm projector.

Arnold recalls, "There wasn't an actor alive that could resist buying a picture of himself acting . . . I made a lot of money. It cost me about seventy-five dollars; I charged them three-hundred fifty for it." In this way Arnold taught himself the rudiments of filmmaking.

Arnold was appearing in the huge Broadway hit *My Sister Eileen* when the Japanese struck Pearl Harbor. The very next day he set about getting himself enlisted as a cadet for pilot training. Concerned that he might be a little underweight, he had his mother sew lead weights into his clothes. Expecting to be called up right away, he gave notice at the theater and was given a hero's farewell. Over three weeks went by, however, and he still had not been called. Angry and out of work, he made inquiries at Army Headquarters on Church Street, but was told that his class would not be called for months due to a shortage of planes. Too embarrassed to show his face back at the theater, he wasn't sure what to do. He found his thoughts turning more and more to film, and wrote a few scenarios for patriotic short subjects, which he submitted to various persons including celebrated publisher Clare Boothe Luce. She received Arnold's material warmly and described it as having "passion and lilt," but nothing more came of these efforts. At last, however, Destiny called. Arnold ran into a friend on Broadway, a fellow actor who was aware of his interest in filmmaking—who had, in fact, paid six hundred dollars for two of his "highlight" shorts. He told Arnold to go to Astoria; the Signal Corps had taken over the old Paramount studio and was looking for cameramen. Arnold was thrilled by the possibility, but felt a bit un-qualified. After all, he was entirely self-taught and his experience was limited to 16mm. To remedy this he enrolled in a crash course in cinematography at the New York Institute of Photography, a little private outfit run by an old-timer who had been in business since the early silent days. There Arnold got his first experience in 35mm with an antiquated hand-cranked Bell and Howell. He felt this was not enough, however, and availed himself of a young acquaintance whose father owned the Camera Equipment Company at 1600 Broadway. There Arnold spent a few hours learning how to take a 35mm Mitch-ell out of its box, mount it on a tripod, thread it, and choose the lenses. With the audacity of youth he then went directly to Astoria and told them he was a cameraman. Although he explained that he was eventually to be called for pilot training, he was given the cameraman's test, which consisted of setting up a Mitchell. This he accomplished with dexterity, having just finished practicing a few

Top: *Arnold practices on a hand-cranked Bell and Howell while enrolled in a cinematography course in early 1942.* Bottom: *Arnold, while assistant cameraman for Robert Flaherty, on the set in the old Paramount Studio, Astoria, New York.*

hours before. He was given a civil service rating as an assistant cameraman and was told to report back to the studio the very next day.

He arrived fully expecting to be assigned to a unit making films on venereal disease or how to clean an M-1 rifle, but to his great surprise was told that he was assigned to assist Robert Flaherty, the renowned documentarist. Arnold had been an enthusiastic admirer of Mr. Flaherty for many years. "When they told me Robert Flaherty needed a cameraman, it was like telling me that God needed a cameraman." He was sent to York, Pennsylvania, where Flaherty was making a film under the auspices of the Signal Corps and the State Department to encourage home industry for the war effort. Resolved to tell the truth about his civil service rating, he knocked on Flaherty's hotel door and introduced himself.

There stood this big man, a wonderful looking man, a big Irishman with a shock of grey hair and an aquiline nose, a very imposing looking man. He looked just like what I thought he would look like—you know, God. . . . I said, "I'm your new assistant cameraman." He said, "That's nice." I said, "It might not be so nice, do you mind if I tell you a story?" . . . I told him the story and he laughed and said, "Well, it's not black magic. Don't worry, and if you have any questions, ask me." He was wonderful, he treated me like a son. I stayed with him: My class wasn't called for six months. It was a course in cinematography I couldn't have paid for. He took me under his wing and taught me everything I knew.

He asked me to shoot a sequence on the York Fair. I said, "What do you want, Mr. Flaherty?" He said, "You make it up." He gave me an Eyemo, which is a hand-held 35mm camera, and about three thousand feet of film, and said, "Go out and get me a sequence."

York, Pennsylvania, is Mennonite country—beautiful country. It is like time has stood still. The men still wear those black hats, with bonnets for the women. The children dress just like the adults. They don't listen to the radio or drive cars, just horse and buggy. They're a Calvinist sect. They paint their windows and barn doors blue when they have a marriageable daughter. Fascinating people.

There was a Mennonite family that drew up in a horse and buggy near the fair; I surreptitiously photographed them. They had a little girl about four years old dressed just like her mother, with the bonnet. I took a lot of close-ups of her, using a long lens. As soon as I got enough footage of the Mennonite family, especially the little girl, I went and took shots of the fair using the widest angle lens I had. I told the story of the fair through the eyes of this little four-year-old Mennonite girl, everything looked much bigger. I used an 18mm lens. Everything looked big, immense, like a child would see things.

I brought it back to Flaherty, we had it developed and watched it in the projection room. Afterwards he said, "Come here," and took me to this room. I had never seen a moviola before. He started to break the film down, and cut the sequence together. It was magic. I thought, "I shot that?" He took what I shot and began putting it in dramatic form. He took a quick shot of this and a shot of that, then cut away to something else that I had shot . . . I had shot everything, but he *selected* what I shot. He put it together in such a way that I was amazed by it. It was an education. . . . I learned everything there was: the cutting room, special effects, preparing the film for the lab. He tried to get me out of the Air Corps, but he couldn't get me out because it was the one branch of service—the Air Training Command—where they wouldn't transfer anyone out.[1]

He left Flaherty's unit after eight months with great reluctance, and soon found himself a pilot in the Air Corps. This was not entirely without its bright side, however. Not only did this fulfill his long-standing ambition to fly, but while stationed at Truax Airfield near the University of Wisconsin at New Rochelle, Arnold and his companions would occasionally find their way to the campus in search of the fair sex. It was there that Arnold met his future wife, Betty, a drama student and daughter of a well-to-do dairy rancher. Married after Arnold's discharge in 1944, their honeymoon was unusual. Fredric March (whom Arnold had met in *The American Way*) had just offered Arnold a part in the Theater Guild Stock Company production of *A Bell for Adano*, and the newlyweds spent their first weeks together on tour with the play in New Haven, Boston, and Baltimore.

It was during the run of *A Bell for Adano* that Arnold was visited backstage by Lee Goodman, a buddy from his old air squadron.

He was from a Texas family, a three-card monte dealer and a concert pianist. He was a three-card monte dealer because his family ran a carny in Texas. He studied to be a concert pianist at Juilliard but never forgot how to deal three-card monte. He made a fortune in the Army dealing three-card monte. He came backstage one night, dumped out his money belt and said, "Let's go into business." As it happened, I had just been asked to recommend someone to make a fundraising film for the Jewish

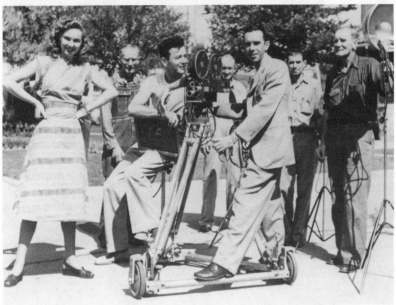

Top: *Arnold (left), as Sergeant Trapani, and Everett Sloane in the Broadway production of* A Bell for Adano, *about 1945.* Bottom: *Arnold (center, with camera) and his wife, Betty, on location in Denver, Colorado, shooting a promotional film for the Jewish Consumptive Relief Society.*

Consumptive Relief Society, now the City of Hope. They had a hospital in Denver, and wanted a film to raise money with. I was going to recommend someone Flaherty had introduced me to in New York, a documentary filmmaker named Lou DeRochemont for whom I had directed a few films. I said, "To hell with Lou DeRochemont, we'll do it. We're just in business, we're going to make a film." So we formed a company. We picked a terrible name, Promotional Films Company. But we made the film and it won a prize. I directed and my wife and I played the leads. It was a dramatic story about a guy who suddenly got tuberculosis and how he was cured. Then we started getting contracts from the Agriculture Department. We made a film called *Chicken of Tomorrow.*

Although over thirty other contracts followed, including films for the Jewish Consumptive Relief Society and most big advertising companies on New York's Madison Avenue, Arnold continued to work in theater. He appeared, for example, in the Broadway revival of *The Front Page,* directed by its co-authors, Ben Hecht and Charles MacArthur. In 1948 he found himself cast by producer Hunt Stromberg, Jr., as the cat burglar in the Boston premier of *Three Indelicate Ladies* starring Bela Lugosi and Elaine Strick.

The following year Arnold and Goodman made a little film for a local of the International Ladies' Garment Workers' Union. This brought them to the attention of David Dubinsky, then president of the ILGWU, and a public figure of national importance. Dubinsky conceived a public relations film that would tell the story of the union through the eyes of a retiring cloakmaker. In Dubinsky's words,

> This is the story of a cloakmaker . . . and the story of a cloakmaker is the story of America. This cloakmaker built our country no less than the people who made the railroads and the people who pioneered through the wilderness. This cloakmaker pioneered through another wilderness, the wilderness of industrial relations, and with courage and sacrifice he found the right way, the American way. So our hero's name isn't Kit Carson or Daniel Boone, and he hasn't got fringes on his coat . . . his name is Alexander Brody, and he likes to play pinochle![2]

Dubinsky initially wanted the film for the ILGWU Golden Jubilee Convention to be held in Atlantic City, where it was screened for 1,100 delegates on May 23, 1950. "And of course it was David Dubinsky's show—his very own. He ushered people to their seats, he saw to it that they all had programs, he gave the cues for the dimming of the house lights, he made sure the drinking water was well-iced, he shushed the latecomers and glared at them for being late."[3]

Afterwards Dubinsky negotiated a theatrical world premiere at the Gotham Theatre on Broadway, where *With These Hands* opened on June 15, 1950. From there it went into a general theatrical release. The following year the State Department's Information Service ordered more than eighty prints for free distribution throughout Europe as part of the overseas campaign against Communism. Release prints were made available in six foreign languages, in both dubbed and subtitled forms.

For the screenplay Arnold approached Morton Wishengrad, a writer close to the labor movement. The story follows the history of the union as seen through the eyes of a retiring cloak operator who is applying for his pension. Flashback episodes include the bitter strike for recognition in the summer of 1911, and the Triangle Shirtwaist Company fire, in which 146 women died because they were locked in the sweatshop. Another sequence dramatizes the struggle to resist Communist domination in the disastrous strike of 1926. The cloakworker then reviews the union benefits: better working conditions, fully equipped health center, Unity House mountain resort vacation center, and the security of the retirement pension system.

Arnold cast the picture with leading Broadway actors: Sam Levene and Arlene Francis as Alexander and Jenny Brody, and Joseph Wiseman as DeLeo, a consumptive Italian unionist. Performances were excellent. Arnold himself appears as a Communist agitator arguing with Brody.

Critical notices were generally good, though the sponsored, propagandistic nature of the film was hardly ignored. Trade reviews recommended the film for release in highly industrial neighborhoods. According to the *New York Times*, "*With These Hands* is essentially a documentary film which extols the many advantages to the members of the I.L.G.W.U. And while these advantages are beguiling and are effectively demonstrated in human terms, they are not the stuff of which successful theatrical entertainment is made. Neither does the picture have sufficient dramatic sweep to render it more than an impressive document for trade unionists."[4] The *Motion Picture Herald* called it ". . . propaganda of a most palatable nature," and hastened to add that "Jack Arnold as the director, and Lee Goodman as producer have done their jobs well."[5] Other reviewers were

Arnold (center) during shooting of With These Hands. *Co-producer Lee Goodman appears just to the left of Arnold behind the camera; the film's star, Sam Levene, is behind Arnold to the right with his arm on the shoulder of the film's editor, Charles R. Senf.*

even more sympathetic, judging the film to be "... a warm and tender drama" and "a masterpiece in its field."[6] "*With These Hands* has ... fine dialogue and warm humor in the screenplay by Morton Wishengrad and an exceptional sense of the dramatic captured by director Jack Arnold."[7] The film was a success, and Arnold found himself nominated for an Academy Award.

The nomination of *With These Hands* surprised and delighted Arnold, but he had no idea how to respond and made no effort to promote the film amongst Academy members in the Hollywood community. In his naiveté he didn't know that it was standard practice in such circumstances to take out ads in *Variety* and maybe rent a billboard or two. *With These Hands* might very well have won in its category, but when the voting came no one had ever heard of it.

On the rooftop set of Girls in the Night *(originally titled* Night Flowers*),
young lovers Hannah and Joe (Patricia Hardy and Leonard Freeman) share
serious moments while Jack Arnold (crouching below the lights just to the
right) directs.*

The nomination did, however, bring him to the attention of
Hollywood, where he soon signed a contract with what was then
Universal-International. After a brief period of apprenticeship he was
assigned to *Night Flowers,* an original story and screenplay by Ray
Buffum. The story deals with poverty and delinquency in New York's
East Side, a locale that Arnold knew very well. (This is partly why
Arnold was chosen for this project, as a certain amount of location
work was planned.) *Night Flowers* was intended to be a melodrama
with elements of romance, suspense, and action. Underlying these
elements is the belief that the dream of a better life can become a
reality. The moral point is also made that our greatest misfortunes
are of our own making and that evil brings about its own destruction.
The murder and suspense angle evolves naturally and logically from

Top: *Although this photo purports to be a "scene from* Girls in the Night," *it is a posed publicity still; nothing this lurid occurs in the film, but the studio was determined to make the most of the exploitation potential.* Bottom: *Also ripe for exploitation, this actual scene from* Girls in the Night *shows Georgia (Joyce Holden), a strip-teaser's daughter, emulating her mother for an East-Side teen social club.*

Two scenes from Girls in the Night: *at top, Chuck (Harvey Lembeck) upbraids Vera (Jaclynne Green) while Hannah (Patricia Hardy), Joe (Leonard Freeman), and Georgia (Joyce Holden) look on. At bottom, Irv (Don Gordon) is about to rob and murder Blind Mimosa (Paul E. Burns) as Vera (Jaclynne Green) looks on in this highly atmospheric and suspenseful sequence.*

the relationships and characters established in the first reel. There can be no doubt that Mr. Buffum was quite clear as to his objectives.

However, the executives at U-I had their own ideas about *Night Flowers*. It was intended to be sold as a "dualer," a "B" movie and a teen exploitation picture at that. There were elements in the story — the beauty contest, Georgia's wild dance number, Hannah and Vera clawing at each other on the street — which were eminently suitable for an exploitation campaign. For the release a more sensational title was chosen: *Girls in the Night*. Arnold did not like this choice because, in his opinion, it cheapened the picture.

Nevertheless, he made the most of the material, approaching the project with great sincerity. "It was a better film than it was supposed to be," says Arnold. "They set out to make an exploitation film just like AIP does today . . . with the girls. . . . But that's not what I set out to do." When seen today, the dialogue, styles, and mannerisms may seem somewhat unnaturalistic and dated, but the film is so well crafted and "of a piece" that one can hardly imagine it any other way. Everything fits together.

The story revolves around three young couples. Handsome Joe Spurden wants to marry local beauty contest winner Hannah Haynes, while Hannah's brother, Chuck, is enamored of Georgia, whom we meet doing her "specialty" dance for "the guys" at a "sorority clubhouse." All share the desire to improve themselves by leaving the East Side for the greater opportunities of Astoria. The third couple, however, Irv Kelleher and Vera "Ugly" Schroeder, have lost any such dreams and have embraced the decay and moral depravity of the inner city. Irv is a switchblade and gun-carrying hood, while it appears that Vera may be an addict. Out of a desire to better themselves (Joe has promised Hannah that he would get enough money to marry her and move to Astoria), Chuck and Joe conspire to burglarize the shack of Blind Mimosa, a fake blind beggar rumored to have thousands of dollars hidden away. Vera overhears their plans and gets there first with Irv, but they are surprised by Blind Mimosa. Irv panics, draws his .32 caliber, and shoots Blind Mimosa to death. Irv then flees back to the poolhall to establish his alibi, while Vera stays to hide the evidence. As she is leaving she spies on Chuck and Georgia as they enter the shack and make away with the money (unaware that Blind Mimosa is dead).

The next day the local cop on the beat and a homicide detective (portrayed as a warm-hearted professional) ask questions but have little to go on. Vera, jealous of Irv's occasional interest in Hannah, now has a hold on him, as only she knows he is guilty. She is also greedy. Revealing to the other couples that she saw Chuck and Georgia steal the money, she threatens to implicate them in the murder unless she is liberally paid off. Putting two and two together, our kids realize that Irv and Vera must have killed Mimosa. Hannah, pretending an estrangement from Joe, goes off to offer herself to Irv in the hope of getting information. As she is about to get in Irv's car, Vera—furiously jealous—claws her to the sidewalk and a fight ensues. When the girls are pulled apart, Vera threatens to expose Irv "for what happened last night" unless he stays away from Hannah. This is all the confirmation Hannah needs. Our young heroes confront Irv as he is about to silence Vera permanently, and a breakneck chase ensues. Chuck pursues the villain through a cluttered waterfront to an old warehouse. While making a final attempt to escape along a narrow building ledge and catwalk, Irv accidentally jumps onto high voltage lines and is dramatically electrocuted. Evil destroys itself. An epilogue completes the happy ending, as the Haynes family moves to Astoria.

Much of the charm of *Girls in the Night* is due to its wholesome naiveté. "We've become much more sophisticated," says Arnold:

> I'm not sure it's for the better. . . . If I were to do a story about that age group, those kids living in that slum today, it would be completely different, though the external conditions are much the same. Yet *we* hadn't lost the dream . . . there's always Astoria to go to. . . . But we found out there isn't any Astoria. [We believed] that if you worked hard—the work ethic—and you were honest and good to people, things would be fine. The cop on the beat was a sweet human being. . . . You'd have a hard time selling that today. [Also] the hero—the knight in shining armor—has almost disappeared. We don't have heroes. I was thinking of [Martin Scorsese's] *Taxi Driver* done in the same kind of genre though he was older, not a teenager, but a young man. Those things existed then but we didn't see them.

Compared to *Girls in the Night*, the moral point of view in *Taxi Driver* is quite ugly and unredeeming.

In spite of the studio's exploitation intentions, *Girls in the Night* provided Arnold with numerous opportunities to assert his creativity. A good city slum mood is achieved, due in part to his thoughtful location choices. Visually, the film has many fine moments. An almost surreal image occurs near the beginning when Kovac, the local cop, steps in front of the screen in a movie theater in order to announce the start of the beauty contest. However, a western is still playing on the screen as he attempts to quiet the crowd, resulting in the bizarre and humorous image of a tiny policeman being trampled over by a stampede of giant cattle. Georgia's dance sequence is realized to very entertaining effect, as are the suspenseful doings at Blind Mimosa's shack. The chase sequence is very exciting, with excellent location work. It starts on and under the Brooklyn Bridge and continues through real New York waterfront locations until the characters cross over a garbage barge and hop a fence into a coal truck. The coal truck was actually in a Long Beach, California, lumber yard; it is there that Irv's shocking demise takes place in a highly effective and satisfactory manner.

This last sequence presented one difficulty: The young actors had some hesitation about running along a narrow walkway at such a dangerous height. Arnold promptly climbed up first, cheerfully demonstrating that there was nothing to it. He got the shot he wanted.

Arnold was not the only newcomer on this picture. The leads were all young hopefuls who, like Arnold, had just been put under contract by the studio. Patricia Hardy, who played Hannah, had recently won a local beauty contest like the character she portrayed. Harvey Lembeck (Chuck) and Don Gordon (Irv) began long careers with this picture, the latter playing mostly heavies as in *Girls.* Leonard Freeman (Joe) gave up acting for producing, eventually becoming very successful with the long-running television series *Hawaii Five-O.* Jaclynne Green (Vera), whom Arnold remembers as a lovely girl and gifted actress, had trouble getting parts and disappeared from the Hollywood scene.

Girls in the Night was released in Los Angeles as the bottom bill with U-I's Technicolor western, *The Lawless Breed,* starring Rock Hudson. It received mixed reviews, some of them unkind. Some reviewers seemed to be annoyed with the producers for being purveyors of exploitation, taking it out on the film. However, *The Hollywood Reporter* called *Girls in the Night* "... a solid little melodrama of New York's slum district that will strengthen any double bill and in some situations, because of its fine exploitation potential, will prove strong enough to stand by itself. . . . Jack Arnold . . . makes his first megging stint a successful one, bringing out consistently excellent performances from his cast and setting a brisk tempo that develops suspense and still allows plenty of comedy relief."[8] The *Motion Picture Herald* said, "The audience at Loew's Commodore in Manhattan, where it was 'sneaked' last week, had a rousing good time all the way."[9] The studio was more than pleased with Arnold's work, and promptly moved him on to bigger and better things.

Unfortunately, *Girls in the Night* is almost never revived today, and appears only rarely on television.

2
Jack Arnold Explores
the Third Dimension

The emergence of commercial television in the late 1940s had a devastating effect on the Hollywood film industry. By 1952, theater attendance had dropped to two-thirds of its 1946 level. Activity at the major studios was reduced by more than half. It was a grave crisis, and the search was on for something that would attract audiences back to the theater. One possibility was first previewed for the press in 1951. *This Is Cinerama*, a film by Arnold's former mentor Robert Flaherty, demonstrated Fred Waller's three-strip Cinerama process. The giant screen filled one's peripheral vision and, with the addition of stereophonic sound, an illusion of depth was created. *This Is Cinerama* was released in the fall of 1952 and generated considerable excitement in the press and public. From a commercial standpoint, however, there were problems. The potential cost to exhibitors for the installation of giant screens and new projection equipment was prohibitive.

Another system, Natural Vision, was designed to use existing screens and, with slight modifications, standard two-projector systems. Developed by two brothers, Milton and Julian Gunzburg, it was a simple two-camera, two-projector stereoscopic system using polarizing filters on projection lenses and viewing glasses. The system was ignored by major studios until independent producer Arch Oboler used it for his infamous *Bwana Devil*. Released in September, 1952, it was a huge success with the public, if not with the critics. The union of mediocrity and box-office success caught the attention of the major studios, and the 3-D rush was on. Warner's

Many of Arnold's films have enjoyed considerable popularity in Europe. The advertising art above is from the German release of It Came from Outer Space.

began with production of *House of Wax*, and was followed by Columbia, MGM, Paramount, and Universal-International.

U-I began production of its first 3-D production, *It Came from Outer Space*, in January, 1953. Jack Arnold, science fiction buff since his teens, was assigned to direct and brought production to a timely conclusion for release in May. It was a smash hit, the biggest picture of the summer, drawing record crowds through June and part of July. It still enjoys an excellent reputation. It is revived occasionally and shows frequently on television. Specialist critics regard *It Came from Outer Space* as a landmark in science fiction film, and a classic of its genre.

The story is unusual. An alien ship accidentally crashes to Earth during a peaceful voyage to another world. The aliens wish only to make repairs and leave, but are discovered by an amateur astronomer who hopes to understand them. Unfortunately, he brings the aliens to the attention of the townspeople, who become hostile and set out to destroy them. However, with a little help from the astronomer, the aliens make a last-minute escape in their ship. The aliens—hideous monsters to us—are wholly sympathetic; the real horror is the fear and hate in the hearts of the intolerant humans. Jack Arnold recalls:

When I got the assignment to direct *It Came from Outer Space*, it gave me a real opportunity, first of all, because it was a story by Ray Bradbury, whom I respected and whose stories always had some meaning and substance to them. The main point was that we are prone—all of us—to fear something that's different than we are, whether it be in philosophy, the color of our skins, or even one block against another in a big city. Because your form is different than theirs you want to hate, you want to kill. That is your first reaction. Until we are mature enough to meet something different than ourselves on a higher level without being afraid of it and without recoiling in horror . . . only then will we be worthy to meet whatever else is out there in the cosmos, and there must be people out there. One must remember also the era in which this film was made. This was the height of the McCarthy era when we were running scared of everything and you didn't have to be a communist to be suspect. It may have been the worst period this country has ever gone through. The whole political climate was one of a witchhunt. And if there were important things to be said about our society and its mores, they certainly weren't being said in the film-fare at the time. So that was the kind of thing I wanted to express, especially in those political times we were living in. We could do it, and get away with it, because it was fantasy. On the face of it, they wouldn't relate it to the problems of the day—those who weren't keen enough intellectually and especially those who were running the studio. They were only interested in the special effects and whether the picture would sell or not. And since I claimed to be a science fiction and effects expert, and there were no experts and no one around to contradict me, the studio left me alone and it turned out to be a good film that made a lot of money. From then on I made all their science fiction films. And the more of these films I made the better I liked it because the studio left me alone and didn't argue with me, no matter what I did. . . .

In addition to being the first 3-D science fiction film, *It Came from Outer Space* marks the beginning of U-I's remarkable science fiction series, and was the first 3-D film to be released in the then new "wide-screen" 1.85:1 aspect ratio. It was also the first film based on a story by Ray Bradbury, and had a considerable effect on the style of subsequent films of its genre, especially in the atmospheric use of Southwest desert locations and the introduction of the "type" of the '50s science fiction hero.

It Came from Outer Space is also remarkable as one of those rare films in which the final result is an improvement of a good idea. In spite of a few minor interpolations and misunderstandings in the screenplay by Harry Essex, the shooting script and film are a definite refinement and development of the original story. The aliens had originally been conceived as lizardlike creatures with the power to alter our perception of them. In the final realization they are actually able to transform themselves into any shape, thus implying the ultimate primacy of mind over matter. The film's distinctive visuals are due in part to the fine art direction of Bernard Herzbrun and Robert Boyle, the beautiful studio "desert" set being particularly noteworthy. The conceptions of the alien ship and the aliens themselves, while simple, are excellent, and have hardly been surpassed for their aura of believable otherworldliness. However, it is Jack Arnold's orchestration of these elements, his imaginative use of locations, and faultless eye for composition, that give *It Came from Outer Space* its power and sustained eerie atmosphere.

The most powerful moment in the film is when amateur astronomer George Putnam (Richard Carlson) first comes face-to-face with an intelligent being from another world. He descends to the bottom of the steaming impact crater, stands before the great dome-like ship, and apprehensively approaches the open hatchway. The next shot is from inside the ship from the alien's point of view: *We are the alien.* We approach the hatchway, see Putnam outside, but back away (in fear?) and slowly shut the heavy door in his face. Yet as audience we also identify with Putnam through his facial

It Came from Outer Space. *At top, George Putnam (Richard Carlson) gazes awestruck into the doorway of the alien spacecraft. Jack Arnold handles this scene from the alien's point of view, leaving something to the imagination and heightening the scene's realism. Below, Putnam stands before the alien spacecraft (by means of a simple and ingenious miniature). This eerie, atmospheric shot is the reverse-angle of the shot of Putnam above.*

Ellen's alien double (Barbara Rush) lures Putnam (Richard Carlson) out into the desert in this scene from It Came from Outer Space.

expressions, those of a man experiencing something beyond the limits of his understanding. Arnold involves the audience's imagination; there is no visible alien to interfere. Moreover, he carefully builds up the sense of atmosphere as Putnam descends into the crater in order to aid suspension of disbelief. Never has the interplanetary meeting of minds, with its profound implications, been portrayed with such subtlety and conviction.

The power of this sequence is not evident in the script, where it is presented in a bare, schematic form:

63   INT. SPACESHIP AT PANEL—SHOOTING OUTSIDE TOWARDS PUTNAM. The mist in front of the lens, suggestive of something looking out at Putnam.... We hear the strange music again, like pinpoints . . . behind it darkness. Now the music

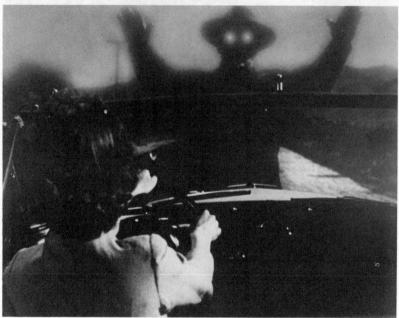

It Came from Outer Space. *At top, Richard Carlson and Barbara Rush pose on the forced-perspective "weather cover set" built in Stage 12, Universal's largest. The rising column of smoke was painted onto the photograph by a studio publicity artist. At bottom, Ellen (Barbara Rush) stops her car for Frank's alien double in this back-projection shot. The glowing eyes were added to this still by the publicity department and do not appear in the film.*

is louder and all around us, almost a whispering. CAMERA
MOVES UP CLOSER TO THE OPEN PORT AND HOLDS.
Now Putnam looks up into the hatchway. As he does so, the
hatchway starts to close.

Another very strange and compelling sequence involves an
alien, in the form of Putnam's fiancée Ellen (Barbara Rush), who
lures Putnam across desert hills to a deserted mine shaft. He sees her
first on a slight prominence, her black evening gown and scarf caught
in the desert breeze. The image is ". . . arresting and beautiful, but
ominous, charged, with menace."[1] She might be a modern-day Circe.
Putnam calls to her, but she runs, disappearing beyond the crest of
the hill. When he reaches the crest, however, she is near the next—
too far away for her to have run in the time just passed. The eerie and
frightening implication is that she only appears to be Ellen while we
(and Putnam) are looking at her. Comparison with the script reveals
that the effect of this sequence is due primarily to the personal vision
of the director. The scene is masterful, on a level with Welles or
Hitchcock.

It Came from Outer Space contains numerous examples of
Arnold's confident and inventive mise en scène. A particularly clever
example takes place on the "desert" set. (Built on Stage 12, the largest
on the lot, the set used forced perspective to create the illusion of a
distant horizon.) Putnam and Ellen have stopped at the side of the
road because they thought they saw something. From the alien's
point of view, we watch them as they leave. The car drives out of our
peripheral vision as we (the alien) step slowly toward the road and
turn to watch the now distant car moving off toward the horizon.
Amazingly, this is accomplished in one continuous shot. As the alien
moves toward the road, the car (now off-camera) goes behind a large
boulder. When the alien turns to look down the road, the camera sees
the perspectivized road, ever diminishing to a false horizon. A tiny
toy car moves up the miniature road. It is an audacious and successful
illusion.

Although Arnold had relative control over It Came from Outer
Space, there were definite limitations. "In those days," he recalls,
"films were made on very strict budgets. . . . Time was also an element. There was only a certain amount of time I could utilize my
energies in fighting for what I wanted in the film, and I had to make
compromises." A case in point is the appearance of the aliens.

Arnold had hoped to avoid a "horror movie" look by relying mostly on shots from the aliens' point of view. The studio, however, had constructed a cyclopean monster to tie in with the advertising campaign.

> I never wanted to show it, I only wanted to use its point of view . . . I only wanted to show a flash, something indefinable in the mineshaft when Carlson confronts it. . . . But the studio, in all the science fiction films we made, were always looking for something exploitable. . . . They wanted something for the three-sheets and the ads. So they came up with "the eye." I balked. I was against it but I shot it, thinking that I would be able to cut it out . . . but the studio insisted on having it in. I wanted to keep it to a minimum, just the suggestion of something. It was a trade-off, letting me do what I wanted to do for the body of the film, which I thought was more important than the one shot of what the alien being was supposed to look like. I figured I came out ahead anyway.

In spite of Arnold's misgivings, the alien is photographed and cut with great restraint, and remains one of the most credible extraterrestrials ever to appear in pictures. It compares very favorably, for example, with the aliens in the 1977 film *Close Encounters of the Third Kind,* who seem like the little children and puppet (for close-ups) that they are.

It Came from Outer Space was produced for about $750,000 — in today's money perhaps $1,200,000. When compared to the reputed $22 million spent on *Close Encounters,* it is evident that Jack Arnold made very good use of his resources. Indeed, in terms of narrative architecture and point of view, *It Came from Outer Space* is the superior picture. If one subtracted the elaborate and costly special effects from *Close Encounters,* what remained would be much like an improvised film school project. The difference between *It Came from Outer Space* and *Close Encounters* is like that between an engraving by Albrecht Dürer and a mechanical billboard on Sunset Boulevard.

It Came from Outer Space is seen often enough on television but is rarely seen in its original format. It was shot in black and white, though some prints are tinted sepia to enhance the desert locations and skin tones. The sound track is stereophonic. The wide-screen, polarized light 3-D image is of very high quality. Some scenes are breathtaking. Arnold helped develop this system with Clifford Stine of U-I's camera department. Technically, the camera was an

An early, unused design concept for the creature in It Came from Outer Space.

improvement over that of the Gunzburgs', which had the cameras at right angles with a beam-splitting mirror. This meant that one image was flopped, necessitating a generation loss to correct it. The U-I system used two Mitchell cameras side-by-side with one upside-down so that the lenses were near each other. The upside-down camera was accordingly altered to run backwards in synchronization

Following page: The studio insisted that Jack Arnold include the "eye creature" in It Came from Outer Space, *even though he felt it cheapened the film. At top, the creature as conceived by the studio publicity department; below, the creature as it actually appeared in the film.*

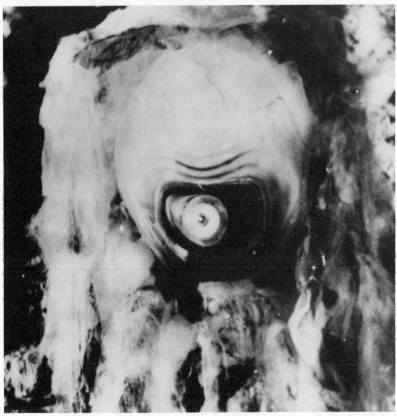

with the other. Arnold took great care in the placement of the interocular point of convergence, which determines whether an object will project or recede from the screen. This is a vital concern in good stereoscopic photography, and one often handled clumsily. Arnold also deserves credit for avoiding purely gratuitous 3-D effects.

For the world premiere at the Pantages Theatre in Hollywood, an additional effect was added. The most startling 3-D shot in the film is an avalanche along the crater wall. Everyone ducks as massive boulders really seem to tumble out of the screen. At this moment Arnold gave the cue to trip catapults set up at the sides of the screen, scattering styrofoam rocks into the audience. "You should have heard them scream," he says.

The screams had hardly died down before the studio assigned Arnold to a second 3-D picture, *The Glass Web,* produced by Albert J. Cohen *(Girls in the Night).* Released the following October as a cofeature with *Walking My Baby Back Home,* it was described in contemporary reviews as ". . . easily the standout of the double bill . . . a good suspense film"[2] and

> . . . another good picture that doesn't need 3-D . . . taut dramatic fare . . . an attractive and efficient production, tightly directed by Jack Arnold, who gets excellent performances out of a fine cast.
> The story has a feminine villain, a cold-blooded, golddigging TV actress, played by Kathleen Hughes, whose tantalizing performance is one of the film's top delights. The ambitious girl is blackmailing an ex-lover (John Forsythe), writer of the "Crime-of-the-Week" TV show, and at the same time bleeding the show's researcher and casting director (Edward G. Robinson), who is envious and jealous of Forsythe and aspires to be a writer himself. When Kathleen is found murdered in her plushy apartment, after having told Robinson in plain words that she's been playing him for a sucker and ordering him out of her life, he tries to frame the killing on Forsythe. But in scripting the headline murder for the TV program, the meticuluous Robinson includes such minute details that he winds up trapping himself as the murderer—and the police catch up with him just as he is about to shoot Forsythe and his wife (Marcia Henderson), whom he has tricked into coming to an empty TV studio.[3]

Arnold very much admired *D.O.A.,* a film directed by his friend Rudolph Maté just four years earlier. The story of *The Glass Web* is not as uncompromisingly black as that of *D.O.A.;* the web of incriminating circumstances that threatens the hero is eventually

The Glass Web. At top, Henry Hayes (Edward G. Robinson) pleads with cold-blooded temptress, Paula (Kathleen Hughes). Below, Don (John Forsythe) discovers the strangled body of Paula and realizes he may be implicated as her killer.

Top: *Edward G. Robinson threatens the lives of John Forsythe and Marcia Henderson in the final reel of* The Glass Web. Bottom: *Relaxing between takes on the set of* The Glass Web *are (left to right) Edward G. Robinson, John Forsythe, Jack Arnold, and assistant director Irv Berwick.*

shattered, he redeems himself, and justice prevails. Yet here Arnold had an opportunity to work in the *film noir* genre, and he set about to make the best of his material and resources. The result, while lacking the relentless intensity of the best of the genre, is a credible entry, with a number of attractive and novel features. The behind-the-scenes look at the world of early commercial television is as interesting to watch now as it was for audiences in 1953 (though for different reasons). Particularly evident is the director's keen appreciation of the many dark ironies implicit in his material. Especially fascinating is the opening where we see bad-girl Kathleen Hughes murdered, only to discover, as the camera pulls back, that we are actually in the television studio witnessing a production of the *Crime-of-the-Week* show. The television announcer doing live in-studio cigarette commercials is quite bizarre, a restrained black humor touch pointing up the crude mercenary mentality behind commercial television. The scenes with Kathleen Hughes are very well staged, providing a perfect setting for her superbly sexy and sinister performance, while creating interesting stereoscopic compositions. Some good suspense (with touches of dark humor) is created when John Forsythe attempts to flee after discovering the body; he must not be seen, but his path is blocked by drunken party-goers who want to involve him in the festivities. As the web of fate apparently closes in, he walks aimlessly though the night on wet, back-lot streets, in the purest tradition of *film noir* imagery.

It is evident that Arnold made every effort to strengthen weak scenes with strong imagery whenever possible. The best example of this is in the scene where John Forsythe drives Edward G. Robinson to the top of an oceanside cliff, possibly with the intention of pushing him off. The effectiveness of the scene is greatly heightened by the dramatic appearance of the cliff itself, an artificial creation conceived by Jack Arnold and realized with the flawless traveling-matte work of Clifford Stine. Matte work was also used to put images on the television monitors. Considering the technical difficulties involved in matting stereoscopic images, the unhesitant and successful employment of these techniques in *The Glass Web* and *It Came from Outer Space* is commendable.

A minor flaw is the inclusion of a few inadequately motivated 3-D effects, perhaps a result of studio insistence. As John Forsythe wanders trance-like through the dark back-lot streets he (1) is nearly run down by a truck (ladders on its roof pop out of the screen), (2)

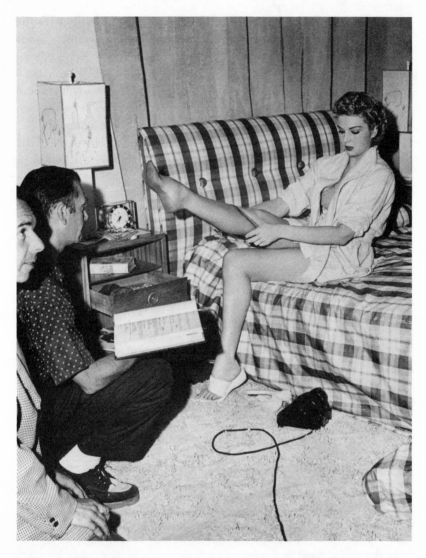

Jack Arnold (far left) directs Kathleen Hughes in an amusing sequence from The Glass Web: *Her leg will project out from the screen in the 3-D version. Assistant director Irv Berwick holds the script.*

walks under a debris chute near a building under demolition (close-up of rubble cascading over us), (3) walks past a man hosing down the sidewalk (the man turns the hose, and his eyes, right at the camera), and (4) is nearly hit by a large bundle of newspapers being thrown off a truck. In a "flat" presentation this seems too much, though in 3-D the near-comedic effect is quite compatible with the dark, ironic tone of the whole. A less objectionable 3-D effect occurs when Kathleen Hughes puts on her nylon stockings, precise adjustment of the point of convergence projecting her shapely leg perfectly out of the screen. While not strictly necessary for the advancement of the plot, the effect is humorous and enjoyable, and serves to further establish the irresistible and fatal charms of the character.[4]

From the director's point of view, *The Glass Web* is particularly memorable for the strange experience Arnold had with Edward G. Robinson:

> Eddie Robinson wasn't a mean man, he was a man with troubles. He had almost been called by the McCarthy committee, he had serious family problems, and he had been blackballed in the industry. *The Glass Web* was his first picture in quite a while, and he had always gotten star treatment. The first shot on the first day of shooting involved him coming down a staircase and crossing right to talk with a beautiful young blonde. I was going to shoot it from a crane, following him down the stairs, moving with him across this big room, and ending up in a tight two-shot. Eddie came on the set, I explained the shot, and he got furiously angry. "What the hell did I do?" I asked. He snapped back, "Mr. Arnold, I'm used to courtesy!" I said, "Mr. Robinson, I wasn't aware that I was discourteous, and if I was I apologize. All I said was that we're going to start up there, pan on you coming down with the crane . . . ." He interrupted, pointing to the right side of his face, "*This* is my best side!" I looked at him in amazement—here was this ugly little guy—and I said, "Mr. Robinson you're beautiful on *both* sides." He gave me a dirty look and walked off the set. He wouldn't come back until we rebuilt the whole set in reverse so we'd be shooting his best side! Eventually I got to know him pretty well; he was a very nice man. My wife and I were invited up to his truly palatial house and got to see his fabulous fine art collection. And I finally found out which was his best side—it was the one without the mole!

In spite of a few plot holes, the storyline of *The Glass Web* provided Arnold sufficient opportunity for interesting staging and visuals. A worthy little thriller, its neglect may be due in part to its association with 3-D. Released in both 3-D and flat versions, it has never been revived in its original format and is rarely seen today.

Arnold's next project, *The Creature from the Black Lagoon,* is regarded by many as one of the best 3-D films ever made. Although

Jack Arnold on the set of Creature from the Black Lagoon, *in the back lot at Universal. Top: Arnold aboard the* Rita *on the back-lot lake. False-front buildings on back-lot streets can be seen in the background. The* Rita *was not a fully functional craft, and Arnold arrived one morning to find it had sunk during the night into the shallow waters. Bottom: Arnold discusses a scene with the cast aboard the* Rita. *Left to right: Whit Bissell, Julia Adams, Richard Carlson, Nestor Paiva, Arnold.*

inspired by the real-life discovery some years before of a prehistoric coelacanth off the coast of Madagascar, the story is less science fiction than pure horror melodrama. Paleontologist Carl Maia (Antonio Moreno) astounds the scientific world by the discovery of a weird fossilized web-fingered hand in the cliffs along the upper Amazon. A team of scientists, Dr. David Reed (Richard Carlson), Dr. Mark Williams (Richard Denning), Dr. Edwin Thompson (Whit Bissell), and Kay Lawrence (Julia Adams) return with Maia to the Amazon to search for the rest of the skeleton. When they arrive at Maia's campsite they discover the bodies of his brutally murdered assistants. Despite this ill omen, they hire a tramp steamer piloted by the superstitious Captain Lucas (Nestor Paiva) and continue along the river in search of fossils, theorizing that the missing bones have been washed further downstream. Unknown to them, their every move is being watched by a mysterious, unseen presence. They eventually arrive at a dead end, the dreaded Black Lagoon, the depths of which may contain the fossil bones they seek. Despite warnings by Captain Lucas (who relates the native belief that the lagoon is haunted by an ancient demon), David and Mark go exploring below in their scuba gear while Kay goes for a leisurely swim on the lagoon's surface. Watching from below, the Gill Man is fascinated by her graceful movements, and imitates her in a bizarre and macabre *pas de deux*. He reveals his presence and great prowess by leaving a gaping hole in an underwater net that had momentarily ensnared him. The struggle between modern man and primeval monster begins, with David hoping to capture the Gill Man alive for study while Mark intends to bring back a carcass that will bring him fame and fortune. Mark succeeds in spear-gunning the Gill Man, who in turn vents his anger by killing a hapless crewman. Captain Lucas then suggests bringing the Gill Man safely up from the depths with "rotinone" powder, a drug used by natives to paralyze and catch fish. They saturate the lagoon with the powdered drug, and the Gill Man eventually floats helplessly to the surface. He is imprisoned below deck, but the drug wears off sooner than expected and the Gill Man escapes after seriously injuring Dr. Thompson, who had been on watch that night. Not underestimating the Gill Man's intelligence, power, and desire for revenge, David convinces everyone that they must flee the lagoon before the Gill Man returns. To their horror they discover that the narrow passage has been blocked by a huge log—the Gill Man has them trapped. David and Mark team up underwater

An evocative portrait of the Gill Man taken on location in the waters of Silver Springs, Florida.

to move the log; David attaches a winch chain while Mark acts as look-out, spear gun in hand. Mark spots the Gill Man and cannot resist one last attempt to kill him. The Gill Man outwits him, however, mangling and drowning him in the bottom of the lagoon. The Gill Man then returns to the boat, snatches Kay, and carries her off through the murky depths to the entrance of his secret lair. David follows in his scuba gear, and surfaces in the Gill Man's cave to find an apparently lifeless (and ravaged?) Kay draped over an altar-like rock. When he sets his gun aside to revive her, the Gill Man suddenly springs out from nowhere and attacks. David attempts to defend himself with a stone and a knife but to no avail. He is helpless in the Gill Man's grip. Just as the Gill Man is about to kill him, shots ring out. Captain Lucas and his crew have found their way into the cave from its dry land entrance. The Gill Man hesitates between Kay and

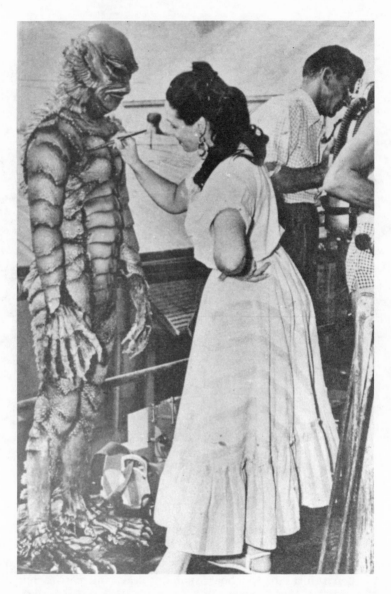

Artist Milicent Patrick, one of the Gill Man's designers, retouches the costume during the shooting of Creature from the Black Lagoon.

the safety of escape into the water, but Lucas and his men continue to fire. Badly wounded, the Gill Man staggers backwards into the water and plunges into its depths. He is last seen sinking motionless through the vegetation in the bottom of the lagoon.

Though occasionally dismissed as minor and derivative sensationalism by insensitive critics, more recent and informed appraisals have recognized *Creature from the Black Lagoon* as a classic refinement of venerable mythic archetypes, brilliantly reinterpreted for its age. Undoubtedly, this accounts in part for the film's continuing popularity. Equally undeniable is that, while many fine talents contributed to its creation, it is the personal vision and directorial verve of Jack Arnold that gives *Creature from the Black Lagoon* its peculiar dynamic appeal.

Arnold was involved with the project from its very inception, working with producer Alland to evolve the story and sell the studio on the idea. His storyboarding and additions to the shooting script were made with a keen intuitive awareness of the psychological mainsprings that make real horror work. In fact, there are few examples in the cinema where the language of mythic archetype is pushed so far and used with such clarity. Arnold recognized in *Creature* an opportunity to work in an idiom that draws its inspiration from the deepest levels of our psychic life. It was a chance he did not waste.

A penetrating analysis by critic Frank D. McConnell elucidates the meaning of the film, and establishes its importance as a work of art "brilliant in its truth to its form and era."

> Unlike any other monster one can think of, he is the result of no cause, neither accident nor devilish science nor the supernatural: he simply *is*, primal and eldest, and the outrage he generates is the curse only of those unlucky enough to discover his existence. . . . The action of the film, then, is the story of what happens to those who seek out—and seek to capture—the primal secrets which are *there* all along in the innocence and blandness of their unharassed privacy. . . . A strange film, a strange blend of insight and inadvertence of the archaic and post-industrial . . . a film, a work of art, which like all major works of art makes sense only by making sense of its age. *Creature from the Black Lagoon* confronts, as frankly as 'fifties reticence will allow and more subtly, perhaps than 'sixties and 'seventies frankness can manage, the tangled skein of sexual, social, and violent impulses out of which politics is made.[5]

McConnell's essay is thought-provoking and well worth reading, but it is by no means necessary for appreciating the film. *Creature from the Black Lagoon* is a wonderful movie; one responds automatically to its atmosphere, eros, and 3-D thrills.

The film also established its real star, the Gill Man himself, as a redoubtable personage of modern mythology. He is the only monster since the thirties to attain the kind of universal recognition accorded such venerable bogies as Dracula, the Frankenstein Monster, and the Wolfman (with the possible exception of his gigantic Japanese cousin, Godzilla). There are few people today who don't know what the Gill Man looks like, though many may have never seen his films. In addition to his appearance in the two sequels (Revenge of the Creature and The Creature Walks Among Us), he is known from countless toys, posters, masks, and model kits. In the 1955 film The Seven Year Itch, Tom Ewell takes Marilyn Monroe out to a movie—Creature from the Black Lagoon. Emerging from the theater Marilyn comments, "I felt so sorry for the Creature. . . . I think he just craved affection." A 1957 calypso song by Lord Melody told the sad tale of a boy taunted for having an ugly father, none other than the Creature himself.

The Gill Man began to take shape during the production of It Came from Outer Space when producer Alland came across a story by Maurice Zimm and called Arnold in to help him develop it. Working with writers Harry Essex and Arthur Ross, they succeeded in selling the story to the studio, and pre-production began. The question then naturally arose as to the Gill Man's physical appearance. Arnold recalls wondering, "What the hell was this guy going to look like? I had this little plaque from when I was nominated for the Academy Award; it had this little Oscar on it. I began to imagine what he would look like with a fish head and fins. So the make-up department went to work on sketches and the costume itself. . . ." Artist Milicent Patrick did most of the sketches, with design contributions by Jack Kevan, Bud Westmore (head of make-up), and Chris Meuller, Jr., who did the original clay sculptures of Arnold's fish-headed, fish-finned Oscar.

Arnold began scouting for a location that could double for the mysterious lagoon, a search that brought him at last to the Silver Springs resort area in the Florida Everglades. There he saw the elaborate water show featuring, among other attractions, a number of young women on water skis. One of these performers was hired to double for Julia Adams in the underwater scenes. It was at this time that Arnold met young Ricou Browning, a student at Florida State and a swimmer in the water show who could hold his breath for an amazing four or five minutes. Browning was showing the Universal production people some possible locations when Arnold asked him to do some swim-throughs for a camera test. Arnold was so impressed

Top: *Director Jack Arnold (right), swimmer Ricou Browning (in creature suit), and crew on location in Silver Springs, Florida, for* Creature from the Black Lagoon. Bottom: *Browning (right) and crew members on location for* Creature.

Top: *Ricou Browning (in creature suit) poses with Julia Adams' swimming double and underwater camera operator Scotty Welborne, on location for* Creature from the Black Lagoon. Bottom: *Underwater camera work for* Creature. *The camera is a unique 3-D dual Arriflex designed by Universal effects wizard Clifford Stine.*

by his performance that he hired Browning to play the Gill Man in all the underwater sequences.

Browning was brought back to Hollywood, and the making of the Gill Man began in earnest. A good deal of experimentation was required, and the early suits were not that successful. "Some of the first costumes were pretty funny," recalls Arnold. "One of them was like winter underwear and stretched like crazy when we got it in the water."

The final suit was an elaborate affair of cast latex foam. Its creation required taking a plaster cast of Browning's entire body over which the Gill Man was sculpted in clay. A plaster mold was then made of the finished sculpture. After the clay was removed, the latex was poured into the space between the body cast of Browning and the mold of the Gill Man; the whole assembly was then baked in a kiln until the latex was "cured." The completed costume was essentially one piece, zippered up the back, with separately cast hands and head secured by snaps. The result was impressive but excessively buoyant in water. To keep Browning from constantly bobbing to the surface, lead pieces were sewn into the legs, and Browning was equipped with a form-fitting vest and belt of thin lead weights. Several copies of the suit were made and painted differently. The suit used for underwater photography was painted yellow to increase its visibility, while the suit seen out of the water was painted green. Another green out-of-the-water suit was prepared for stunt man Ben Chapman, taller and more robust than Browning (but lacking Browning's aquatic skills), who portrayed the Gill Man when on land.

Browning recalls the great difficulty he had performing in the final costume, which he likened to "swimming in an overcoat." Another problem was seeing where he was going. There was no room for goggles under the rubber head, and the little peep-holes in the Gill Man's eyes were about an inch away from Browning's own. Nonetheless, Browning gave a truly masterful performance. He did every shot while holding his breath, getting more air when needed from an off-screen hose without surfacing. "When we were filming," recalls Arnold, "he would signal me that he needed more air by going completely limp. Then he'd swim over to this air hose, then swim back into the scene and we'd continue filming." The illusion that we are watching a genuinely aquatic creature is quite convincing. An additional touch of realism was provided by the make-up department, who equipped Browning with a squeeze bulb with which he could

Creature from the Black Lagoon. *The Gill Man watches in fascination as Kay swims gracefully above him; moments later he secretly joins her, swimming below her and imitating her movements in a macabre* pas de deux.

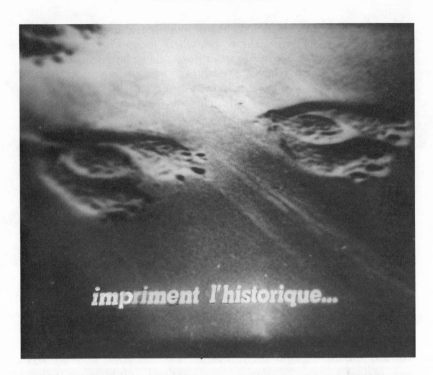

In an eerie prologue to Creature from the Black Lagoon, *Arnold visually establishes the course of prehistoric evolution by means of a series of cross-dissolved footprints on an ocean beach. This still is from a subtitled French print of the film.*

pump air into the Gill Man's gills so that they would flex and flutter convincingly in close-ups.

The portrayal of the Gill Man is a true *tour de force* due to inspired design, the underwater skills of Ricou Browning, and the sensibilities of the director. With location work in the Everglades, a back-lot lake, and a few simple sets, Arnold surrounds the Gill Man with an atmosphere of mystery and subtle beauty that has been likened to the masterworks of Cocteau.[6] Particularly memorable is the sequence in which the Gill Man contemplates from below the graceful beauty of the heroine as she swims above him. It is both frightening and highly erotic. Innocent and virginal in her white bathing suit, she unselfconsciously displays her luscious sexuality in an improvised water ballet. In the murky depths below, the fascinated monster mimics her with his own brutally masculine movements.

I wanted to create a feeling of mystery and romance—but also a sense of terror. The scenes where the girl is swimming above while the monster watches from below play on the basic fear we all have about what might be lurking below us in the water. Being scared of something unseen is basic to our nature. If a piece of seaweed brushes your leg you might scream and swim like crazy—you don't know what the hell is under there.

It was also just beauty and the beast, the primeval urge of the male for the female. But people who see Freudian metaphors here may be giving me too much credit. I was happy that it did turn out poetic. I made sure to shoot it with the sun directly overhead so the girl was almost in silouette. And it came out much the way I wanted it, which is rare. . . .

But I wanted to make the Creature—"my little beastie" as I called him—a sympathetic character because I liked him. Here he was being chased and killed in his own environment when he just wanted to be alone. He was only violent because he was pro-voked to violence. So we were trying to say something about human nature, though not in a polemical way—in a way that would be entertaining and acceptable to an audience.

The excellence of Arnold's underwater work owes much to the fine cinematography of James C. Havens, made possible by a unique dual-Arriflex 3-D camera designed and built by effects wizard Clifford Stine. Arnold's figures and objects move through an eerie three-dimensional space with no limit, giving these scenes an extra-ordinary dreamlike quality. White clouds of powdered sedative seem to explode in slow-motion spirals through the plane of the screen. Bursts of shimmering bubbles boil up from the inky depths below.

The film has many other attractions. Especially impressive is the opening prologue in which Arnold contrives to show us a pyrotechnic creation of the world in spectacular 3-D, followed by an ingenious se-quence depicting the evolution of life from the primordial ocean. The ebbing waves reveal strange little footprints of some unseen prehis-toric creature; then, through a series of dissolves, the footprints change and grow until they are those of the monster we meet later in the film. These last prints are accompanied by a distinctive musical "stab" which is later used throughout the film as the Gill Man's *leit motif.* The sequence as a whole is cinematic, atmospheric, and highly effective. It is also a resourceful and economic way to make the in-tended story point—what could be cheaper than footprints on the sand? Another magnificent image occurs after the Gill Man has ab-ducted the heroine to his lair; the hero finds her limply draped over an altar-like rock in the midst of a subterranean grotto. Arnold invests this scene with an aura of primeval power. The script is also quite good; though basically a horror melodrama, it is well structured, with succinct, fluid dialogue. It also makes a few ecological and philosophic points while never being pedantic. The cast is enjoyable and perfect as the types represented.

Made for less than $650,000, *Creature from the Black Lagoon* made millions after its release and inspired the studio to make a sequel, *Revenge of the Creature*. "The Creature was such a sensation," says Arnold, "that the studio wanted us to do a sequel right away. So we got together — the producer, the writers and I — and said, now what? The only natural thing to do was capture him and bring him back alive. We put him in the big aquarium tank at Marineland." The relative success of *Revenge of the Creature* is due naturally to elements borrowed from the first film, but there is an added interest; the tension between the primeval being and civilization is thrown into much higher relief. The Gill Man is drugged, captured and put on display in Florida's Marineland oceanarium, where a pretty blonde icthyologist (Lori Nelson) attempts in vain to train him. These scenes of the Gill Man's oceanarium captivity are well directed and photographed, and have a strange, haunting quality. We cannot help feeling for the Gill Man as he endures the humiliating ordeal of being chained to the tank bottom and "trained" with electrified prods — to the amusement of gaping onlookers. There is a reprise of the swimming scene in the first picture, with a variation. The Gill Man watches the girl swimming above, but as he is about to grab her, her lover (John Agar) takes her into his arms and kisses her as the Gill Man looks on — considerably heightening the sexual tension. Escaping his tormentors, the Gill Man shows nothing but violent contempt for our (to him) alien world of metal, glass, and concrete. Yet it is hard not to have a certain sympathy for the Gill Man, and the analogue to one's own relationship to society is clear.

The Gill Man's escape from the oceanarium is truly thrilling cinema and provides for some well-motivated 3-D shock effects. After breaking his chains, the Gill Man leaps from the pool with astonishing, almost supernatural force. This was accomplished by equipping Browning with a harness and yanking him out of the pool with piano wires as he approached the surface. Before it becomes apparent that he is dangling helplessly, there is a cut to another angle, this time at the edge of the pool with the water beyond. In this shot

SC. 284 JOE & GILL MAN GRAPPLE
UNDER WATER!

SC. 284 GILL IS PULLING JOE
—WITH POLE— INTO TANK
DOWN SHOT

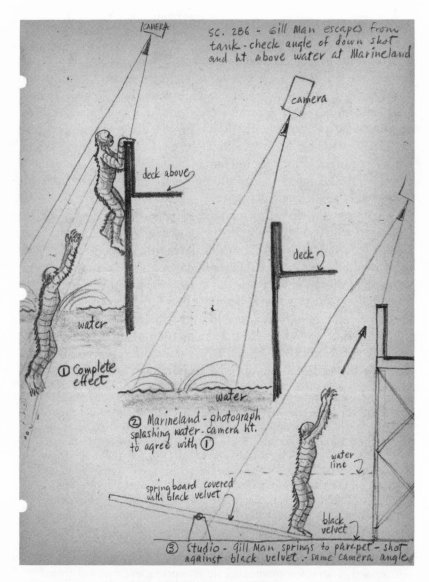

SC. 286 - Gill Man escapes from tank - check angle of down shot and ht above water at Marineland

camera

deck above

deck

water

① Complete effect

water

② Marineland - photograph splashing water - camera ht. to agree with ①

springboard covered with black velvet

water line

black velvet

③ Studio - Gill Man springs to parapet - shot against black velvet - same camera angle

Opposite: *Storyboards* (top) *from* Revenge of the Creature, *and a still* (bottom) *from the actual scene, with John Bromfield as oceanarium attendant Joe Hayes.* Above: *A pre-production drawing showing a proposed effect for the Gill Man's oceanarium escape in* Revenge of the Creature.

Browning crouches just out of sight at the pool's edge and pulls himself suddenly up into the camera. The two shots are cut together at precisely the right point, and the effect is awesome and frightening in 3-D. Moments later, as the Gill Man runs amok, there is an amusing shot of a life-size display cut-out of the Gill Man being knocked over into the audience's lap by fleeing patrons—followed seconds later by the Gill Man himself. Another highlight occurs when the Gill Man breaks in on a teenage jam session, scattering "cool cats" all over the place. Even more fun is the scene where the Gill Man creeps up on Miss Nelson through her bedroom French doors as she sits before her dressing table in her negligée. There is a close-up of the Gill Man here, dripping wet and gasping for air like a fish out of water, that is very effective. An abduction and ravishment follows, with some excellent (and eerie) night-for-night cinematography.

Arnold's favorite story about the making of *Revenge of the Creature* has to do with shooting the key scenes at Marineland. When he was scouting the location he was shown the big oceanarium tank filled with all manner of dangerous sea creatures including sharks, barracuda, moray eels, a sea turtle, and an octopus. There were divers who went down into the tank and fed them by hand. After looking the situation over, Arnold asked the Marineland people if they would screen off half of the tank with a net and segregate the dangerous fish from the actors. He explained that he was not only shooting the Gill Man but also the leading man and lady.

> I knew they'd take one look in the tank and refuse to get in. So the Marineland people promised me they'd arrange for a net. I returned some while later with the production company to get ready to shoot—there was no net! I said, "Where's the net?" They said I didn't need a net because the fish were too well-fed to bother the actors. So I had a little problem. How the hell was I going to get my actors to go in there? Now as it happened, I had this really nutty cameraman on that picture who didn't mind swimming around in there with the sharks. He talked me into going into the tank with him to show everybody how safe it was. So I put on a diving mask and scuba tanks and jumped in with my eyes closed. After a few moments I slowly opened one eye and about a yard away there was this goddamn shark at least twelve feet long looking straight at me. I didn't know what the hell to do so I just froze. It moved slowly toward me and brushed against me as it passed. Its skin felt awful, like sandpaper. After the shark moved off I came up and said "Nothing to it, fellas!" The joke is that by the third day everyone was actually kicking the sharks out of the way. The only problem we had was with this big sea turtle that wanted to eat the Gill Man's suit and kept biting chunks out of it. Once he bit the whole heel off so I assigned a grip with a club whose only job was to keep the damn turtle away from the Gill Man.

Revenge of the Creature also has the minor distinction of marking Clint Eastwood's debut in motion pictures. Arnold cast him in a small role as the lab assistant with the white rat in his pocket.

He was shy and self-effacing; little did I realize he would someday be a star. When I told him I was going to put the white rat in his pocket he said softly, "You are?" I said, "Don't worry, it won't hurt you." I used him again in a bit as one of the jet pilots that destroy the giant spider in *Tarantula!* I also worked with him on the television series *Rawhide.* He told me that he had been offered the lead in that Italian western that made him a star. I told him, "Take it, for chrissake!" I liked him very much and was happy to see him find such success.

While *Revenge of the Creature* may lack the thematic purity and gothic atmosphere of the original, it is nonetheless a creditable effort that enjoyed such popularity that the studio wanted yet another sequel, this time *The Creature Walks Among Us.* By now Arnold had no desire to do another Creature film. He felt that he would only be repeating himself at best and that it would be difficult for him to equal his previous efforts. But he did think it would be a good opportunity for his assistant director, John Sherwood, to step up to director. Arnold feels that *The Creature Walks Among Us* is the weakest film of the three because the two previous films had already explored every aspect of the Gill Man's personality and relationship with humans. In defense of the film, however, it may be pointed out that *Creature Walks* is in some respects a different kind of story from the other two, perhaps not to be compared to them. It is less an adventure and is more brooding and existential. The film's subtext is also somewhat different in the statement it makes about our relationship with nature and the ends of applied science.

The release of *Revenge of the Creature* in March 1955 marked the end of an era; it was the last Hollywood 3-D film produced in the 1950s. "The demise of 3-D," observes Arnold,

wasn't a failure of technique but of showmanship. Properly exhibited, the 3-D effect of these films is superb. But projecting 3-D is tricky business. If the projectors are a frame or two out of synch it will tear your eyes out. We had our guys in the main houses to make sure there was enough light on the screen and the shutters were synched. But by the time we made our third 3-D picture all the smaller studios were making them too, and they didn't have the manpower to supervise the exhibitors. People got headaches, and the studios gave up on 3-D.

The end of 3-D was hastened by the introduction of CinemaScope in 1954, which offered a spectacular, if quite different, effect with none of the problems of 3-D.

Revenge of the Creature has, in recent years, regained a certain popularity after being televised in anaglyphic (red/green) 3-D. This process, however, is so inferior that it is likely to do as much harm as good to the film's critical reputation.

3
Infinitesimal and Infinite

The most celebrated of Jack Arnold's science fiction films is *The Incredible Shrinking Man,* and justifiably so. Based on a story by Richard Matheson, it is yet another example of a good story greatly improved by the storyteller. Arnold's clear, straightforward storytelling is at its best here, but even more important is his penetration into the deeper implications of the story's premise and the relentless logic with which he brings the story to its only possible conclusion.

The film opens with Scott Carey (Grant Williams) and his wife Louise (Randy Stuart) sunbathing on a small cabin cruiser adrift on a bright sea horizon. Their conversation and manners convey an uncomfortable boredom. While his wife is below, Scott confronts a strange low mist that sweeps over him and vanishes as it came. He is covered with sparkling particles that soon evaporate. His wife thinks nothing of it, and within a few days he forgets all about it.

Later he is accidentally sprayed with an insecticide while driving. Again, he suspects no great harm, but within a few days he discovers his clothes seem larger than they had before. He realizes something is wrong. His gradual alienation from his familiar, conformist existence is at first darkly humorous. His former lifestyle is a stylized caricature of American bourgeois values; he and his wife are blonde, the walls of their house white, he is, until he loses his job, an advertising executive. His consultation with medical experts suggests the ultimate impotency of scientism to explain the secrets of man and nature. His wife reassures him that she will support his struggle as long as his wedding ring stays on his finger; a moment later it falls off. As his normal relations with the world dissolve away, he becomes a freak, an object of notoriety, of perverse human interest.

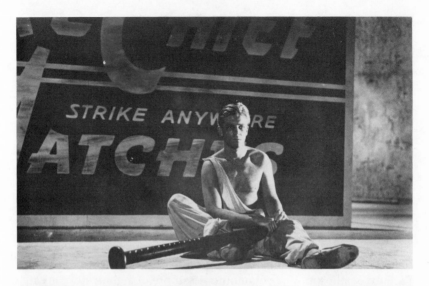

The Incredible Shrinking Man. *At top, Grant Williams as Scott Carey contemplates his fate beside the matchbox that becomes his temporary home. At bottom, a frame still from one of the well-executed split-screen effects. A sharp eye may follow the split down along the right edge of the left-hand curtains, around the small side table, and straight down across the floor. A slight discontinuity of the curtains and the baseboard is visible under the side table. Randy Stuart, left, is Scott's distressed wife.*

Science provides a remission, and a brief encounter with a pretty side-show midget temporarily eases his self-pity; but he continues to shrink. We next see him apparently normal-sized, as if all had been a bad dream, but soon discover that he is smaller than ever and living in a doll-house. The cat, seen first as little more than a possession, a household ornament, and later as Carey's companion, is now his greatest adversary. In a frightening and humorously macabre episode, Carey barely escapes being gobbled up only to fall from the bright, orderly middle-class interior into the filth and dirt of the basement below. His wife believes him eaten, and his last ties with the human realm are forever severed. In another touch of black humor, a newscast describes his "death" as due to a "*former* house-pet."

The central sequence of Carey's life in the cellar is riveting; the philosophical notion of "worlds within worlds" is conveyed with visceral intensity. Arnold succeeds where philosophers and theoretical physicists fail because he *shows* us what they only talk about — thus turning familiar surroundings into a merciless, relativistic environment. Carey's former life and identity gone, he sets about trying to survive in a dark, alien environment where ordinary objects are transformed into a surreal landscape, a more perfect realization of the aesthetic world explored by Duchamp and Oldenberg. Ironically, the tiny man is now more like a mythic hero. His final confrontation with a (to him) giant spider is the high point in the film, and indeed one of the great moments in cinema, reminiscent of Siegfried's encounter with the dragon in the film by Fritz Lang. In a moment of apocalyptic intensity, Carey spears the spider with a pin and, like Siegfried, is bathed in the monster's vital fluids. Siegfried sought by this means to make himself invincible; Scott Carey, too, is changed by this horrific baptism. He arises from his ordeal no longer hating the monster, no longer desiring food. Beyond attachment and desire, he steps through a basement grating (formerly too small for him) into the garden outside. As he gazes upward at the stars his internal monologue reflects on his enlightenment, his final liberation.

I was continuing to shrink, to become
— What? —
The Infinitesimal?
What was I? Still a human being?
Or was I the Man of the Future?

If there were other bursts of radiation,
Other clouds drifting across seas and continents,
Would other beings follow me into this vast new world?

So close.
The Infinitesimal and The Infinite.
But I suddenly knew they were really
The two ends of the same concept.
The unbelievably small
And the unbelievably vast
Eventually meet.
Like the closing of a gigantic circle.

I looked up,
As if somehow I would grasp the heavens.
The Universe,
Worlds without number,
God's silver tapestry spread across the night.
And in that moment I knew the answer to
The riddle of The Infinite.
I had thought in terms of Man's own limited dimension.
I had presumed upon Nature.
That Existence begins and ends, is Man's conception, not Nature's.
And I felt my body
Dwindling . . .
Melting . . .
Becoming nothing.
My fears melted away
And in their place came . . .
Acceptance.
All this vast majesty of creation,
It had to mean something.
And then I meant something, too.
Yes, smaller than the smallest.
I meant something, too.
To God there is no Zero.
I still exist.

The film concludes with these words, soaring inspirational music, and images of galaxies, worlds without end.

One can hardly speak of Jack Arnold's *contribution* to *The Incredible Shrinking Man;* to the extent that such a thing is possible in an intrinsically collaborative medium like film, it is *his* movie. Arnold was regarded with some deference as U-I's science-fiction expert, and received little interference from producer Albert Zugsmith, who had little idea what the project was all about. The only problem was

A *Christlike Carey moments before his transcendental apothesis in* The In-credible Shrinking Man.

with regard to the film's ending. To anyone casually familiar with the works of Lao-Tzu or Plotinus the ending is logical and edifying, but this was not the case with the studio executives:

> The studio wanted a happy ending. To the studio executives a happy ending meant that the doctors find a serum to reverse the shrinking process, Carey is reunited with his wife, and they live happily ever after. I had quite a to-do with them, as such an ending is not at all right for this film. I wouldn't stand for it — I refused. While we were shooting the ending, Grant began to look Christlike to me. There was a certain mood and impact created as he climbed through this little grate he could not get through before;

The Incredible Shrinking Man. Top: *Scott Carey (Grant Williams) is attacked by his former house pet—now a hideous monster. The cat was enticed to ferocity by the presence of a small bird just out of frame; Williams was matted in later by Clifford Stine. Stine's technique did not provide Williams with shadows, but the matching of perspective and synchronization of movement is almost perfect.* Bottom: *The cat reaches through the dollhouse window to strike down Scott Carey in this highly expressionistic image.*

the whole atmosphere is religious — deliberately so. I decided I
wanted a kind of metaphysical ending; it was based on my own
personal religious feelings, my ideas about God and the universe.
I may be a minority of one, but I think what we did with this
scene — and the way Grant Williams played it — was highly effective. In my opinion it is visual and cinematic. Anyway, Universal
trusted me and said, "Let's test your ending." The first preview
went so well they decided to release the film with my ending, and
it was very successful. Some people were shocked by the ending,
however, and there are still some who don't like it. They felt that
the ending came somewhere out of left field, but many liked its
poetry. For better or worse, I take the credit — or discredit. The
ending was entirely my idea.

And so it is. Mr. Matheson's novel (and screenplay) has no such ending; the conclusion, such as it is, implies only the possibility of continued adventure in ever smaller realms. Mr. Matheson rejected the
film for many years as a result of this and other changes, notably the
restructuring of the story from his original flashback format. As Jack
Arnold points out today, a straightforward, picaresque narrative is
the only way such a fantastic story can be told; a flashback structure
would only antagonize an audience and ultimately lose their interest.
Credit for much of this must go to screenwriter Richard Alan Simmons, who did the rewrite, but did not take credit at Mr. Matheson's
insistence. All parties agree, however, that the film's unique ending
is due to Jack Arnold's persistence and inspired imagination.

It is a quest for the meaning and limits of human identity.
Carey learns about himself, human nature, and the nature of the
universe — and learns to accept his fate. As he dwindles almost to
the size of an ameba, Carey begins to unlearn his past. Hunger
disappears, he thinks more clearly than he ever has before, his
mind is bathed in white light, and he feels a new source of inner
power independent of food and a physical body. The tremendous
irony of *The Incredible Shrinking Man* is that Carey's maturity
comes only when he is reduced to the tiniest of creatures. To in-
herit the universe, he must know what it is to be *truly* meek. . . .
The root of Matheson's story was what the bomb did to one
man. Everything else, his changing relationship with his wife and
the other persons and objects around him, came from that. The
challenge as a director was to make you believe that a man could
shrink down to less than an inch, then finally disappear into
nothing. This was broken down into stages. We began by using
clothes that were several sizes too big. We then skipped down to

Here and on following page, a few of Arnold's storyboard sketches showing one of Scott Carey's early encounters with the spider in The Incredible Shrinking Man.

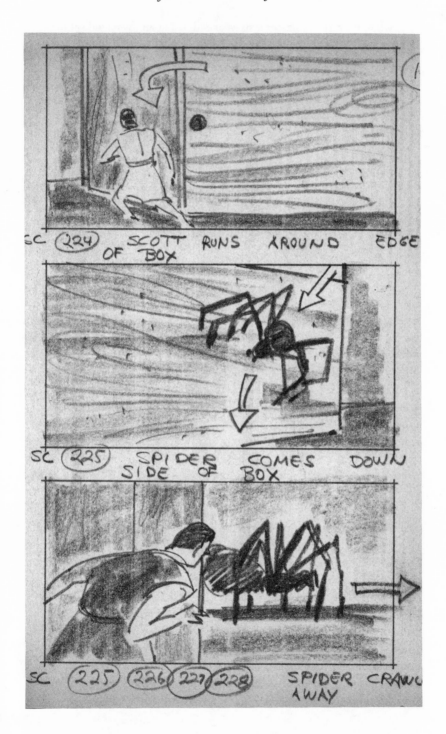

SC (224) SCOTT RUNS AROUND EDGE OF BOX

SC (225) SPIDER COMES DOWN SIDE OF BOX

SC (225) (226) (227) (228) SPIDER CRAWL AWAY

when he was the size of a six-year-old, using an oversized set for Grant, combining this by means of a split-screen with the normal set so that his wife and he would appear together in the same shot. The matte line was hidden along the edge of the curtain, around the side of the chair and down to the floor so it wouldn't be noticed. There were a few little mistakes here—the furniture was a bit off and the phone was too big—but it worked pretty well. We next went down to six inches, in the sequence where Carey is living in the dollhouse and is attacked by his pet cat. The shot where the cat shoves its claw through the dollhouse window was particularly difficult. I got a shot of the cat fiercely reaching out for a little bird that was just off camera and back-projected it through the window. I also had a giant fake paw that I could stick in and out fast. I might add that while the bird was needed to get the right reactions from the cat, we were very careful that the bird was never harmed. After the cat knocks Carey down into the cellar I used a combination of gigantic props matted together with normal-sized ones—and of course the spider. . . .

Artistically and technically *The Incredible Shrinking Man* broke new ground and, while technical effects have advanced somewhat since, for sheer impact it has few equals. Effects that are good enough not to disrupt one's suspension of disbelief are preferable to highly glossy effects that attempt to make up for a lack of story. Moreover, if one considers that *The Incredible Shrinking Man* was made for about $700,000, the effects are very good indeed. The key was in the meticulous planning, the director himself storyboarding each sequence. The careful integration of giant props, back-projection and matte work was worked out in every detail. Examination of Arnold's original storyboards reveals him as no mean draughtsman, and the many striking visual compositions in the film are all there.

Working closely with camera expert Clifford Stine, Arnold devised a simple and ingenious method of matching elements to be matted together. They began with the spider sequence, as it posed the greatest challenge. In this sequence, the spider and the tiny man are not only seen together but react to each other and appear to come in contact. The effect was achieved by first shooting the spider on a normal-sized basement ledge set. The story required Carey to confront a black widow spider, but a real black widow was too small to photograph. "You couldn't keep it in focus. We had to use a larger spider and of course tarantulas don't build webs, either. But I took dramatic licence that it was just sort of a generic spider." Even the domestic tarantulas were a bit too small. In order to have sufficient

The Incredible Shrinking Man. *At top, the spider crawls onto Carey (Grant Williams) as he reaches for the off-screen pin that will save him. The superbly synchronized matte work was a collaborative effort of director Arnold and effects wizard Clifford Stine. At bottom, Carey has a mild flirtation with an attractive sideshow midget, Clarice (April Kent, actually a normal-height actress). This wide-angle photograph reveals the bottom of the back-projection screen (a few feet behind the outsize table), which is hidden in the actual film by tighter framing.*

depth-of-field to keep the spider in focus, high intensity lighting and a very large spider were needed. Sixty of the largest (nearly six inches across) were flown in from Panama; many were needed as the intense lighting tended to cook them. "Now I had the problem of how to direct a spider. One of the grips came up with the idea of using jets of air, which worked very well." Afterward, the sequence was cut and the spider's movements were carefully timed. In Stage 12, huge sets were built of part of the wall, the spider web, and the basement ledge — large enough that Grant Williams would appear to be only an inch in height. The camera was then positioned about two hundred and fifty feet away in order to match the perspective of the original scene. Precise matching was accomplished by inserting bits of negative from the first scene in the gate of the camera. Arnold worked out a system with a metronome so that, by counting the beats, Williams could move in synchronization with the previously filmed movements of the spider.

> I rehearsed Grant with the metronome. We did it all by numbers. Grant had a different action to perform at every count and had to imagine what was happening at each point. I'd say "Action!" and at each number he knew just what the spider was doing. For eight or ten counts he would shake the web, then the spider would descend for so many counts, and so on. We matched all of his movements to that of the spider, then Cliff Stine and his effects team married the two pieces of film together. And there you had it. Grant really appeared to be there on the ledge with the spider — the illusion was perfect. Cliff was a genius. He worked everything out mathematically. There was no tell-tale jiggling in our matte technique, and we had only one retake due to miscalculation. In a scene where a three-foot-high Carey was supposed to put his arm around his wife, one half of the split-screen was off by just one millimeter and had to be shot over. That was the only mistake in the whole picture.

Scott Carey's date with the side-show midget presented another problem, solved in a completely different way. Arnold sought to avoid the difficulty and expense of additional matting with a clever use of back-projection. A large-scale coffee shop table was placed before the process screen in such a way that Carey and the midget (actually a normal-sized actress) seem to be little people. A real midget appears to walk over to the table and talk to them (and seems to be their very same size) though he is actually on the back-

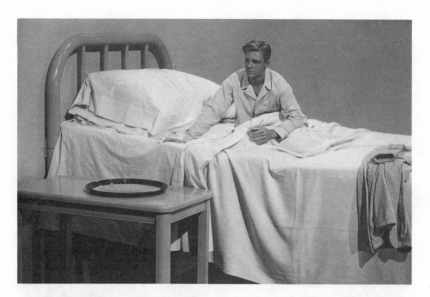

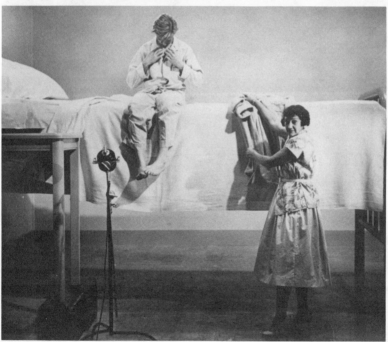

Here and on the next two pages, shots from the production of The Incredible
Shrinking Man *show the giant-sized props and the effect they produced.*
Above: Scott Carey (Grant Williams) *in his hospital bed. The first photograph
shows the scene as it appeared in the film, while the second (with the wardrobe
mistress placing his robe on the bed) shows how the effect was accomplished.
Note the side table brought up to height with boxes.*

Top: *Scott Carey (Grant Williams) warily watches the spider from behind a ball of string.* Bottom: *Jack Arnold directs Williams on the giant basement ledge set on Universal's Stage 12.*

Top: *Caught in a flood from a leaking water heater, Scott Carey (Grant Williams) clings for life to a floating pencil.* Bottom: *Jack Arnold (second from right) watches the filming as Williams clings to the giant pencil.*

projection screen. The effect is not perfect, due to a slight disproportion in the size of the large table, and to the appearance of the girl, who has none of the redundant physiognomic peculiarities associated with midgets or dwarfs. The effect is nonetheless fascinating to watch, and in no way interferes with the story's unfolding.

Another difficulty arose in the cellar sequence, in which the water heater begins to leak. Scott Carey is living in a match box at the time and "large" drops of water begin to fall on the "roof" of the box.

> The biggest technical challenge that confronted me was how to make giant water drops in proportion to a man an inch high. We tried everything, bucket brigades, faucets that turned off and on—nothing looked like an oversized drop! Then I remembered that in my ill-spent youth I found some strange looking balloons in my father's drawer. I didn't know what they were, but they made dandy water bombs. I used to drop them on people off the top of the building where we lived in New York. They had a nice drop shape on the way down and splattered on impact. So I asked the crew if anyone had a condom on him. When one of the guys finally came forward, we filled it with water, tied it off, and dropped it from the top of the sound stage. It had a perfect drop shape, splattered on impact like a drop of water, and was in perfect proportion. I ordered a hundred gross of them and set them up on a treadmill—it worked perfectly. At the end of the picture, the production office called me in. There was one item in the expenses they didn't understand. They asked me, "What the hell was that for?" I said, "Fellows, this was a *very* hard picture, and when it was done we gave a big party...."

The Incredible Shrinking Man is a truly unique accomplishment in the history of film, of which its creator is justifiably proud:

> The only other film to attempt something similar before this was *Dr. Cyclops,* but the people stayed the same size and it did not have the required atmosphere. I wanted to create a mood of what it would be like if you were that small and everyday things that you take for granted suddenly became bizarre and threatening. A pet that you loved—a cat—becomes a hideous monster. A spider becomes the most terrifying thing you've ever seen. I wanted the audience to be in the shoes of this man and feel it as he felt it. I feel that I accomplished this, and that gives me great joy.

But Arnold attributes no small measure of the film's artistic success to the bravura performance of actor Grant Williams. *The Incredible Shrinking Man* posed a range of special challenges. Williams ad-
mirably expressed the most subtle psychological states, as in the
quiet close-up of him studying his bed, registering thereby an eter-
nity of sexless nights. On the other extreme, he was required to perform a variety of demanding athletic actions involving a great deal of
climbing, falling, and struggling in torrents of water. Much of the
time he had to react to beings or objects that were not actually with
him on the set but were added later through matte work. "In that
situation," says Arnold, "a director's only insurance is an actor who
is intelligent and knows his craft. He must have the ability to imagine
for himself what is supposed to be happening in a given scene. For
this, Grant Williams deserves great credit. He had nothing to play
against, yet succeeds in suspending our disbelief. *The Incredible
Shrinking Man* was almost three-quarters silent and required real acting. Grant gave a truly outstanding performance. . . ."

Universal's reluctance to profit from rerelease or video cassette
sales of *The Incredible Shrinking Man* may in recent years have been
due to the intention of making some kind of sequel. John Landis
originally developed *The Incredible Shrinking Woman* and was to
write and direct, but Universal cancelled the project when the
budget was found to be too high. It was later revived by Jane Wagner,
a close friend and associate of Lily Tomlin, the film's star. The resulting film attempted to be a satiric comedy with an ecological message,
and was a disappointment to many. It also had the "happy ending"
that Universal had wanted in the original film, in which the protago-
nist grows big again. Arnold did not enjoy seeing the premise of his
film so casually wasted:

I hated it. There was no point of view and the special effects
weren't even that good. But the major fault is that it's not comedy
even though they tried so hard to make it funny. . . .
I saw a recent revival of the original film a few months ago.
I could hardly get a seat, there were so many young people trying
to get in. It played to full capacity. The audience enjoyed the film
even more than when it was made. They got all the nuances that
I put in. It was a joy to me, just to watch their reaction to the film.
And they were mostly too young to have seen it when it was first
released.

Since its release in February 1957, the reputation of *The Incredible Shrinking Man* has steadily grown. Initially regarded as a routine, if above average, horror thriller, it has come to be regarded as "one of the best science fiction films so far,"[1] "... a fantasy that for intelligence and sophistication has few equals."[2] But it is more than just excellent science fiction or fantasy; it is a good film, directed with great control and persuasion. Its reputation would no doubt be greater and extend, perhaps, outside the circle of science fiction enthusiasts, were it not for the fact that it has not been rereleased and is very infrequently revived or televised.

4

Tales of a
Contract Storyteller

During Edward E. Muhl's tenure as production head at Universal-International, Jack Arnold was but one of seven or so contract directors assigned with various line producers to projects of every genre. Arnold often did not know why he was assigned to a particular script, or what vagaries a property may have undergone before it was handed to him. Yet the process was not wholly random, as evinced by the repeated teaming of Jack Arnold and producer William Alland. Sometimes, as in the case of *Tarantula!*, a director or producer might even originate a project, then gain the interest of production executives. "We were about to have a kid," recalls Arnold, "and I was broke. I knew the studio needed something. At a certain time of the year my driveway used to be covered with tarantulas. They won't hurt you—I've picked up plenty of them—but I knew a lot of people were afraid of them. That's where I got the idea for *Tarantula!*—and I shot it in ten days!"

Tarantula!, based on an original story by Jack Arnold, was an attempt to duplicate the immense success of Warner's 1954 giant ant movie *Them!* It was the fourth effort of the Arnold-Alland team, and one over which they had considerable control. The talents of Clifford Stine also played a significant part, as the effect of the giant spider scuttling over the Arizona desert depended on his expert traveling matte work. Robert M. Fresco collaborated on the story and wrote the screenplay.

One is not surprised to find the story somewhat farfetched. Professor Deemer (Leo G. Carroll), Malthusian biochemist, is working

75

Tarantula! *At top, Professor Deemer (Leo G. Carroll) and his still-growing arachnid before its escape into the desert. Below, Professor Deemer in the final stages of acromegaly, induced by injection of his own experimental growth serum.*

Top: *On location for* Tarantula! *in the Mohave Desert, director Jack Arnold (just below the camera in spotted shirt and turned-down sailor hat) shoots a scene with John Agar and Mara Corday (far right). These rocks were a favorite location of Arnold's and were used to atmospheric effect in several of his films.* Bottom: *The giant spider on the loose in* Tarantula!, *thanks to the fine traveling matte work of Clifford Stine.*

On the back lot during the shooting of Tarantula!, *director Arnold and stars John Agar and Mara Corday examine a few frames of an optical composite showing the giant spider attacking.*

in his desert laboratory on an "atomically stabilized" nutrient to augment world food supplies. The nutrient causes incredible growth in test animals, but sudden gross acromegaly in humans. This is discovered when two of Deemer's assistants try versions of it on themselves. One dies wandering in the desert, the other loses his mind, injects Deemer and smashes the lab. The giant animals escape, including a tarantula with unlimited growth potential. Deemer's lovely new lab assistant, "Steve" (Mara Corday), the town doctor (John Agar), and the sheriff (Nestor Paiva) investigate, and discover that the now giant spider has been eating horses and humans. Agar tries dynamite to dissuade the monster from entering town, but it takes Air Force fighter jets dropping napalm to finally stop it. A happy ending, with Mara Corday safe in John Agar's arms.

The most remarkable thing about *Tarantula!* is that director Arnold manages to bring off such outrageous and contrived goings-on with relative credibility. There are even some very atmospheric scenes, such as at the beginning (under "hairy" credits) wherein a grotesque, dying man staggers through the desert and collapses. Another eerie scene occurs at night when the spider preys on horses at a ranch. Throughout, Clifford Stine's matte work is very good and produces some bizarre and memorable images. Some scenes, while appropriate to the film, are rather funny, especially the shot of the spider's giant face leering through a window at Miss Corday. It seems doubtful that a giant spider would take so much personal interest in her. Also, the grotesque make-ups worn by Deemer and his assistants seem a little out of place, being apparently designed to add an element of human horror, something extra to feature in the publicity. Yet Arnold provides a number of quietly terrifying touches and some truly powerful, dark images, such as the giant spider squatting like a curse over the heroine's isolated desert house. In the final scenes the monster looms so huge over the tiny town as to appear surreal — more metaphor than monster.

The publicity for *Tarantula!* was pretty wild and rather amusing. One ad shows the giant spider with a scantily clad girl in its mandibles; the copy reading, "Can all mankind escape the terror of its dread embrace . . . the awesome evil of its venom-dripping jaws?"

Tarantula! is competent and fun, but not recommended to those who have an intrinsic disinterest in giant "bug" movies. Those who have a taste for such things, however, will most likely find it grand entertainment. The reviewers liked it for what it was and had some fun with it. "All in all, it's a great children's picture — particularly for bad children — as it should scare the hell out of the little monsters."[1]

Tarantula! was not the only story Jack Arnold wrote for Universal; he also co-authored *The Monolith Monsters*, produced in 1957 by Howard Christie and directed by Arnold's former assistant director,

John Sherwood. (Jack had moved on to better things after the success of *The Incredible Shrinking Man.*) Strange meteors fall to Earth and, when in contact with water, grow into towering obelisk-like crystals which crash into fragments under their own weight. Their destructive potential is obvious but they have another creepy effect; fragments lodging in human flesh cause the victims to turn to stone. An original and intriguing idea, *Monolith Monsters* was one of the better minor science fiction thrillers produced by U-I in the late 1950s.

Most of Jack Arnold's films, however, were assigned to him without his prior consultation; he simply had little choice in the matter. Some of these projects were based on quite ordinary material, though many of them are quite good due to his adroit direction. An outstanding example of this is *The Man from Bitter Ridge*, an action western made just before *Tarantula!* Based on William MacLeod Raine's novel, *Tomahawk, The Man from Bitter Ridge* tells the story of Jeff Carr (Lex Barker), a special investigator come to the cattle-town of Tomahawk to get the facts on some stage hold-ups and killings blamed on highland sheepherders, headed by Alec Black (Stephen McNally). After some unpleasant confrontations with the local banker and politician Ranse Jackman (John Dehner) and his gun-happy brothers, Jeff correctly figures just who is really behind the robberies. Meanwhile, a romantic interest develops between Jeff and Holly Kenton (Mara Corday), attractice shepherdess, sparking a serious but sporting rivalry between Jeff and Alec Black. However, Jeff and Alec team up in the end to defeat Ranse and his henchmen in a shoot-'em-up finale, leaving the bad guys dead and Jeff making wedding plans with Holly.

One hardly expects *The Man from Bitter Ridge* to be an authentic depiction of life in the Old West. It is, rather, a popular melodrama—with adventure and romance—well fashioned to meet the expectations of its audience. As such, it is a superb example of its genre and period; one can scarcely imagine how it could be better than it is. The familiar goings-on are briskly paced and expertly staged throughout. The hero and heroine are attractive. The aficionado of fifties popular culture will also be highly entertained by Miss Corday's wonderfully fashionable western attire. Though supposedly the daughter of impoverished sheep ranchers, she sports the latest in ladies' riding gear, her orange-red lipstick in perfect color coordination with her neckerchief. Miss Corday is a delightful screen

Special investigator Jeff Carr *(Lex Barker)* confronts villainous banker and politician Ranse Jackman *(John Dehner)* and his henchmen in The Man from Bitter Ridge. *Left to right: John Harmon, Dehner, Myron Healey, Barker.*

presence, full figured yet petite and refined, who mounts her horse with agility, grace and sensuality.[2]

Reviews were quite favorable. *Variety* noted, "*The Man from Bitter Ridge* has good, albeit familiar, story values and plenty of action.... Cast toppers ... go about the outdoor business ... with assurance under the snappy-action direction by Jack Arnold. Barker is quite at ease with his hero role...."[3] *The Hollywood Reporter* stated that "the film's most notable plus quality lies in the improvement in Barker's acting ability. He is acquiring an ease of manner.... In this he benefits by Jack Arnold's direction, which stresses the casual amid the melodramatic happenings."[4] This "ease of manner" did not come easily, however. As Arnold recalls,

The first day Lex came on the set, I had never seen anyone as nervous as he was. I started to stage the scene we were scheduled to do and he just ran out of the set. So I told everyone to go get coffee and I went over to Lex to calm him down.... He was a wonderful guy, I loved him, I got to know him very well. Lana [Turner] was his wife, she was a big star, and she was coming down to the set later. I had to calm him down and tell him not to pay any attention but to me, "You're only playing to me, nobody else. There's no one on that set but me and I'm your friend, and I won't say print anything if I don't think it's good. Believe me, Lex, you can trust me. I will not print anything that's bad." And I won his confidence. I did a couple takes, and didn't like them, and I told him, "Lex, you're still nervous, you can do better than that . . . ." So I had to baby him along and he was so grateful he gave me a gold tomahawk with a pearl handle. . . . *Tomahawk* was the original name of the western. . . .

Without doubt, *The Man from Bitter Ridge* is one of Lex Barker's best performances.

That same year, just after the completion of *Tarantula!*, Arnold directed another color western, *Red Sundown*, released in January of 1956. It was his first occasion to work with Albert Zugsmith as producer;[5] this was not without advantage as, due to Mr. Zugsmith's relative inexperience in motion picture production, Arnold was able to work with little interference. The result was another superior action entry, in some ways an improvement over *The Man from Bitter Ridge*. This time the plot revolves around the familiar theme of a gunslinger (Rory Calhoun) who wants to give up his old life and settle down. Becoming deputy sheriff, he gets involved in a range war between settlers and a greedy cattle-baron, shoots it out at the end with the cattle-baron's psychopathic hired gun (Grant Williams), and finds happiness with the sheriff's daughter (Martha Hyer).

While the material is once again quite standard, unusual incidents and characterizations help to raise the production above the ordinary, and the controlled energy of Jack Arnold's storytelling unfolds the action at a good pace. A very exciting and unusual scene occurs at the beginning, when an old gunslinger (James Millican) saves the hero's life by sacrificing his own, thus motivating the hero to mend his ways.[6] Desperados have Calhoun and Millican trapped in a remote shack, and set fire to it. The old saddle-tramp buries Calhoun in the shack's dirt floor, with a bit of concealed stovepipe for air. As flames engulf the shack, Millican staggers out at the last

Opposite, top: *Rory Calhoun as Alec Longmire in* Red Sundown *is a picture-perfect Western hero in the high style of the period.* Bottom: *Psychotic gunman Chet Swann (Grant Williams) courteously terrorizes helpless settlers in a suspenseful scene from* Red Sundown.

Top: *Alec Longmire (Rory Calhoun) aids dying gunslinger Purvis (James Milli-can), who sacrifices his own life to save Alec's in* Red Sundown. *Below, Alec Longmire is now Deputy Alec, striking a blow for justice against greedy cattle baron Rufus Henshaw (Robert Middleton) in* Red Sundown's *bare-fisted climax.*

minute and is shot down. The shack burns to the ground, and the bad guys leave, assuming that Calhoun must have been wounded and was consumed by the flames. At dawn, however, our hero raises himself from the earth, as if returning from the dead, and starts off resolved to lead a new life.

Red Sundown also benefits from the bravura performance of Grant Williams, whom Arnold cast as an unbalanced young killer. In one well-written scene, Grant courteously terrorizes a settler's family with truly chilling effect. Jack Arnold always had a great appreciation for Grant Williams, and cast him in his next two films, *Outside the Law* and *The Incredible Shrinking Man*.

> Grant Williams was one of the best actors around. I first used him in *Red Sundown* in which he played a different type of villain, effete and clean cut. He was brilliant. I used him again as the psychotic villain in my next film, *Outside the Law*. I was so impressed by him that when it came to casting *The Incredible Shrinking Man* I asked for him, since we had to use our contract players. But the studio didn't give him the right parts and his career never quite took off. He had the wrong looks for the time and never caught on with the public. Hollywood wanted a Robert Taylor or Rock Hudson, not a blond guy with blue eyes. And he was a bit too pretty for character roles. Universal should have moved him up to the "A" pictures, but they kept him in the "B" pictures. The same thing happened to him when he went to Warner Bros. He got typed—it's happend to all of us in this business at one time or another.

Jack Arnold's next assignment was a real change of pace, a modest little program thriller entitled *Outside the Law*, featuring the talents of Ray Danton, Grant Williams, Onslow Stevens, and Leigh Snowden. Arnold has accurately described this picture as "the quintessence of the 'B' movie."

> Danton is presented as the son of a U.S. Treasury agent (Onslow Stevens). Because his old man neglected him, the boy became a juvenile delinquent, was paroled to the Army and served honorably. When one of his buddies was murdered in the false currency racket in Berlin, his dad brought him back to Los Angeles promising, in the name of the government, a full pardon if the son would uncover the bogus money gang. The trail leads to the pretty widow of the slain soldier (Leigh Snowden) and the boy falls in love with the suspect, which doesn't please Dad.[7]

Outside the Law. At top, undercover agent Johnny Salvo (Ray Danton, second from left at table) begins his investigation by getting to know Maria (Leigh Snowden, left), the pretty widow of a slain gangster, and small-time hood Milo Barker (Mel Welles, right). Below, the final confrontation between Salvo and psychotic gangster Don Kastner (Grant Williams).

She's in the clear, but the importing firm for which she works isn't. Helping to tip the scales in favor of the law is Williams, in the ring and insanely jealous of Miss Snowden. He goes down in a blast of gunfire at the finale.

Danton gets Miss Snowden and the events also bring about a reconciliation with his father.[8]

Jack Moffitt of the *Hollywood Reporter* noted that the familiar Feds versus Counterfeiters story was ". . . apt to seem a bit old-fashioned to . . . lovers of hard-boiled fiction."[9] Indeed, the film seems a throwback to the program thrillers of a decade before. This is precisely its greatest virtue; the director correctly recognized the type of material he had been given, and adopted a style appropriate to it. At a time when the "B" thriller was fast becoming extinct, Jack Arnold made a contribution to the genre that reflects the best of what the "B" thriller had been in its heyday.

Produced by Albert J. Cohen *(Girls in the Night, The Glass Web)*, *Outside the Law* is very modestly produced, not to say low-budget, and interior sets are frequently merely corners. A discerning eye will detect the separate flats from which the sets were assembled. Yet such limitations in no way harm the picture. They are rather elements in the film's lean vitality, urging the director to new heights of ingenuity. The modest dimensions of the project gave even greater opportunities for meticulous planning. Camera movements are particularly well placed, to excellent effect. The bleak back lot and sparse sets are confidently manipulated to produce a mood which perfectly supports the action.

In one scene a car, its driver shot, careers wildly down an alley, smashing into the side of a car parked on the street beyond. The suspense build-up and action in this scene is very well planned, but the highlight of the scene is the crash itself, achieved through an ingenious and cost-saving process shot. The crash is seen from a point-of-view inside the speeding vehicle, a stationary cut-away car in front of a back-projection screen. On the screen appears a shot taken in the back lot, the camera dolly rushing down the alley towards the parked car. At the apparent moment of impact the stationary car is rocked violently, and there is a quick cut to the actual cars on the back lot street, abutted in such a way as to appear collided. It is a clever effect, simple yet dramatic.

Outside the Law is like a clean, efficient, beautifully tooled little machine. Though plain and unadorned, its story is well told, and in a style of filmmaking that has virtually disappeared. It is definitely a stand-out among Jack Arnold's minor films. A contemporary reviewer regarded it as ". . . satisfactory . . . an okay programmer. . . . Under Jack Arnold's direction the pace holds up and develops sufficient interest in what's transpiring over the 81-minute course."[10] *Outside the Law* also provided good experience for Grant Williams and Ray Danton; the former would make *The Incredible Shrinking Man* the following year, while the latter was preparing himself for success in Budd Boetticher's *The Rise and Fall of Legs Diamond* just four years later.

Arnold's next picture, *The Incredible Shrinking Man*, may have begun as an average thriller, but was recognized as something more after grossing over four million dollars in less than two months. Jack Arnold and producer Albert Zugsmith were promptly raised up from the "B" category and assigned to an "A" production, *The Tattered Dress*, in CinemaScope and Technicolor, starring Jeff Chandler and Jeanne Crain.

> Elaine Stewart portrays a wealthy, married socialite who dispenses sex as if it were going out of season. It is her advances that set the stage for the story.
> A bartender, a former small-town football hero, makes a pass at Miss Stewart and tears her dress in the attempt. This arouses Miss Stewart's ne'er-do-well husband to kill the local boy. Into the California desert town comes a famed New York criminal lawyer (Chandler) to defend the rich outsider. Chandler meets the usual antagonisms and prejudices of the small-town mind. By clever courtroom technique, particularly by tripping up the local sheriff (Carson), he wins an acquittal. However, the sheriff, out for revenge, frames the N.Y. invader by getting a femme juror to swear that she had been bribed. This provides an opportunity for a reconciliation between Chandler and his estranged wife (Miss Crain). Defending himself against the bribery charges, Chandler realizes what a travesty he has made of the law in previous efforts to free gangsters and criminals. In winning his own acquittal, he revises his philosophy of life and vows to defend the underdogs.[11]

The Tattered Dress is a well-made melodrama, with good performances and direction overcoming the occasional artificiality of the script. In watching *The Tattered Dress*, it is obvious that it presented few difficulties for the director, with some scenes providing opportunities for considerable directorial creativity. The best example

On location during shooting of The Tattered Dress, *director Arnold poses poolside with bathing beauties.*

of this is without doubt the film's prologue, which is very cinematic, and utterly without dialogue. At dusk, a small sports car, top down, speeds along a winding hillside road, its headlight beams reaching out before it. A close-up of the driver reveals her to be a fashionable blonde in a torn low-cut cocktail dress, an expression of cynical self-satisfaction on her face. She pulls her car into the driveway of a large,

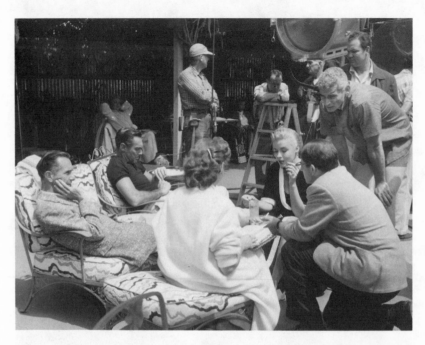

Jack Arnold (far left) goes over a scene with his cast, including Elaine Stewart (in dark robe) and Jeff Chandler (behind Stewart), on location at the big house on Mulholland Drive in the Hollywood Hills during production of The Tattered Dress.

modern ranch-style house and enters through a poolside sliding glass door, which she closes behind her. The door keeps us from hearing the argument that ensues with her husband, enraged by the apparent assault on his wife's virtue. He takes a gun out of a drawer, takes his wife by the arm, puts her in his car, and drives away. We next see a young man, casually dressed, walking alone down a dark street. He pauses before a streetlamp to light a cigarette; as he turns into the light we see the scratches of a woman's fingernails on his cheek. As he draws on the cigarette the husband's car appears around the corner and races toward us. The young man turns to face the car and is shot to death. The car drives on, leaving his body crumpled in the light of the streetlamp. It is a gripping scene, relying entirely on

Opposite: The Tattered Dress. At top, Blane (Jeff Chandler) finds that his wife, Diane (Jeanne Crain), is losing faith in him. At bottom, Super Lawyer Blane is utterly confounded by the emotional display of double-crossing Carol Morrow (Gail Russell) in a gripping courtroom scene.

careful, intelligent staging and camerawork. It is an example of Jack Arnold at his best.

Reviews of *The Tattered Dress* were generally favorable, and U-I had no hesitation in immediately assigning Jack to another star vehicle, this time with producer William Alland *(It Came from Outer Space, Creature from the Black Lagoon)*. Lana Turner had just freed herself from her Metro contract and accepted U-I's offer to co-star with Jeff Chandler in *The Lady Takes a Flyer*. This well-mounted production cannot be taken seriously if it is to be enjoyed. Sterner critics complained about the film's intentions and script, though there was nothing but praise for direction, performances, and technical credits. One of the favorable reviews, that of the *New York Times*, said, "This absurd but adroitly sassy picture is fun from start to finish. One reviewer, who relaxed and had a delightful time, still can't believe it. . . . This handsomely mounted production skips along contagiously, with all the members of the cast obviously enjoying themselves."[12] Years later, in a retrospective review, another *New York Times* critic found the film "surprisingly ingratiating."[13]

The film opens with ex–Air Force Colonel Mike Dandridge (Jeff Chandler) delivering a crippled B-17 to the Burbank Airport. There he meets his best friend, Al Reynolds (Richard Denning), who runs a flight school with aviatrix Maggie Colby (Lana Turner). The three of them form an aircraft ferrying company; Mike and Maggie fall in love during a ferrying trip to Japan, and are soon married. Al, who had hopes of marrying her himself, returns to the Air Force, leaving Mike and Maggie and an ever growing company.

When Maggie becomes pregnant and wants Mike to settle down with her in a house she has rented, Mike insists on piloting planes and leaves Maggie at home with the baby. Enter Nikki Taylor (Andra Martin), one of Mike's pilots, and a raven-haired seductress. In a fit of pique, Maggie takes a ferrying assignment to England, leaving Mike to tend the baby. Mike packs up the baby and succeeds in flying there first, only to discover that Maggie is off-course and having radio trouble. An unsuccessful attempt to land at the fog-enshrouded airport leaves Maggie nearly out of gas; suspense mounts as she attempts to parachute to safety. The cockpit won't open, however, and her plane crashes and explodes on the runway. Mike, a changed man, walks alone on the foggy runway; then he sees Maggie, who had managed to bail out in time, walking toward him. They embrace and attempt to make up.

Top: A behind-the-scenes look at the cut-away cockpit used in The Lady Takes a Flyer. *Left to right at the controls are Jeff Chandler, Jack Arnold, Richard Denning, and Jack Ford, on whose real-life experiences the story was based (crew member behind Arnold unidentified).* Bottom: While ferrying an aircraft to Japan, Maggie, Al, and Mike (Lana Turner, Richard Denning, and Jeff Chandler) develop a love triangle in The Lady Takes a Flyer.

The Lady Takes a Flyer. Top: *Though now a married man, Mike (Jeff Chandler) leaves his wife and child at home and involves himself with one of his pilots, the raven-haired Nikki (Andra Martin). Bottom: With Maggie's plane nearly out of gas and her radio malfunctioning, Mike attempts to "talk her down" in the film's suspenseful conclusion.*

*Jack Arnold assists Lana Turner with her parachute harness in Universal's
Stage 12, here doubling for a fog-enshrouded runway in the final scene of The
Lady Takes a Flyer.*

The story was based on the real life experiences of Jack and Mary Ford, known in flight circles as "the flying Fords." Jack Ford was retained by U-I as a "technical consultant" on the film. Ironically, the Fords were divorced soon after the picture was made.

The Lady Takes a Flyer is a romantic fantasy in the high style of the period. There is about the film a wonderful aura of post-war "American Empire," especially the scenes of Chandler and Turner (in smart pilot uniforms) being served with deference in a Tokyo hotel. Seen from our present perspective, the film's sexual and social values are a bit bizarre and unbelievable, but remain a revealing glimpse of attitudes prevailing at the time. From the standpoint of filmcraft, it is a highly polished example of the best of its day, with above-average production values.

The considerable amount of CinemaScope aerial photography was a welcome challenge for Arnold, who made good use of his experience as a pilot. For the opening sequence where Mike Dandridge lands the B-17, Arnold arranged to have it piloted by a general who was his former commanding officer. Arnold recalls,

> The picture opens up with the delivery of a B-17. . . . We got a general's B-17; the only way we could get it was the general insisted on being the pilot. . . . I don't think this general ever drew a sober breath. . . . They wouldn't let us land in Burbank because we had a charcoal machine, finely ground charcoal to simulate black smoke, and we had to land with two engines out. We had to call the Federal Aviation and get permission. . . . I told them I wouldn't land, but only show him the roll-out at Burbank. . . . I got permission to do the actual landing at the Palm Springs airport. Those days the Palm Springs airport wasn't that busy.
>
> We took off from Burbank, and got very lucky because there were a lot of clouds, we flew about the clouds and got some great stuff. . . . You can't tell speed unless you've got something to judge by.

As the B-17 approached the Palm Springs runway, the engines were cut, and the co-pilot ducked down out of view, putting both feet on the rudder pedal to keep the ship from yawing toward the engines.

> I was in the camera plane, we followed them right into Palm Springs, and got the touchdown. He did a beautiful job. I said, "Okay, let's get some shots on the way back to Burbank where

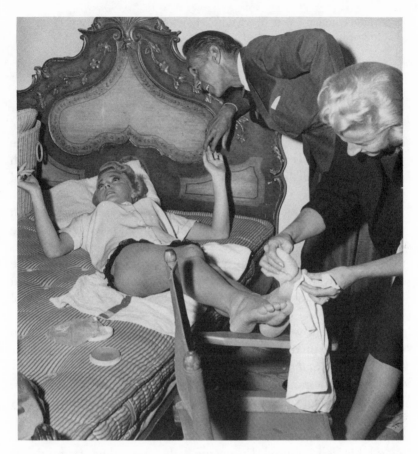

Jack Arnold chats convivially with Lana Turner, who is having her legs painted with pancake make-up prior to a day's shooting of The Lady Takes a Flyer.

we'll take your roll-out." Well, this crazy general turned on the charcoal machine, stopped the props and landed with two props out at Burbank. We had the police, the fire engines. . . . We had everybody, because it looked like a B-17 with two engines on fire, landing at Burbank. . . . I got it on film, but it surprised the hell out of me, I didn't know he was going to do it. . . .

Another beautiful sequence takes place when Mike and Maggie make love in a plane they are ferrying.

The plane was supposed to be on automatic pilot, but of course it wasn't. I was in the C-47 and they were in the DC-3; we had

radio contact. I said, "have fun." They went all over the sky. I had
more fun chasing them over the cumulus clouds.

Arnold got some good performances from his cast. The rivalry
and fight between Jeff Chandler and Richard Denning is good, as is
the romantic chemistry between Chandler and Lana Turner in their
Roman honeymoon suite; Jeff sweet-talks Lana from the ledge of the
bathtub as she bathes. The sequence in which Andra Martin plays the
femme fatale is also well handled; the well framed close-ups with
cocktail and smoking cigarette create the appropriate mood of
sophisticated sin.

Miss Turner, then thirty-seven, required very special attention
with regard to camera angles and lighting, and it is evident that the
director took great care with her shots, which are generally very flat-
tering. Arnold enjoyed the privilege of working with a big star like
Lana Turner, but with this came the unpleasantness of added
demands and studio pressure; the bigger the picture, the less control
he had.

Jack Arnold was assigned, with producer Albert Zugsmith, to
one other "A" picture with Jeff Chandler, on a somewhat smaller
scale than *The Lady Takes a Flyer* and in a considerably more serious
vein. This is the rarely seen *Man in the Shadow*, with Orson Welles.
It is a curious fact that Orson Welles' biographers, at pains to list his
every performance, never mention this film, though it, and not *Touch
of Evil*, was the first Hollywood production he worked on after he
ended his self-imposed European exile. According to producer
Albert Zugsmith, Welles desperately needed $60,000 to pay his back
taxes and took the job without even reading the script.[1]

Arnold recalls getting the assignment to direct Welles in *Man in
the Shadow:*

> I was sitting at the writers' table at the old Universal where the
> black tower is now. The writers turned to me and asked, "You're
> directing Orson Welles, aren't you?" I said, "Yes," and they asked,
> "How are you going to direct him?" I said, "I'm going to do
> whatever he wants!" The first night we were shooting the last
> scene of the film up at this big house they used to have on the
> backlot. They've moved it elsewhere on the lot now; the hill is
> gone now too. It was supposed to be Orson's ranch house, and the
> townspeople were coming after him. Orson was being chased and
> I wanted a shot of him falling. I put the camera in a hole I dug and

Top: *Jack Arnold goes over the script with Jeff Chandler (left) and Orson Welles (second from right) while shooting exteriors for* Man in the Shadow. Bottom: *An enraged Sheriff Sadler (Jeff Chandler, right) forces a showdown with domineering ranch baron Virgil Renchler (Orson Welles) in* Man in the Shadow. *Welles was understandably nervous about working with the guard dog after it attacked a crew member.*

Director Jack Arnold (center) rehearsing an angry exchange between Ben Alexander (left) and Jeff Chandler during production of Man in the Shadow.

wanted Orson to fall over the hole. I told him what I wanted and he just stood there, all three hundred and sixty pounds of him, with those piercing eyes and that voice that goes right through you. Before this we had only met very briefly to discuss the script and wardrobe. This was really the first time we'd had much to say to each other, and I had greeted him like he was the king. He looked at the hole and said, "What's that for?" I said, "Well, as part of the chase I want you to fall over the hole." He looked at me and said, "No, No, it will never work. No good." This was the moment of truth. Was I going to let him step all over me and tell me how to do every shot? I'd rather quit the picture and let him direct! So I said, "Mr. Welles, you're a genius and a hell of a better director than I am, but my name's on this picture. If this is the only shot I make, it's going to be in the picture. So, if you don't mind, sir, we are going to make this shot!" We became good friends after that because I had dared to talk back to him and he respected me.

Hardly anyone would talk back to him and he usually had someone on the set he could pick on.

Another problem cropped up on the same set when Welles was to appear on the front porch with a menacing guard dog. Welles was to threaten Chandler while holding the dog by its chain. The animal was highly trained and appeared quite manageable. The dog, however, had been taught to attack whenever a person raised a forearm to protect his face, and when a member of the crew chanced to wipe his brow with the back of his forearm, the dog attacked him savagely. Welles was greatly shaken and nearly refused to do the scene. At length Arnold managed to reassure Welles, the trainer calmed the dog, and the scene was shot.

> Working with Orson Welles was a remarkable experience. He would take me aside and say, "Look, wouldn't it be a good idea if we did such and such?" It was wonderful—his suggestions were great. I feel sorry for him because he was such a waste of potential genius. He shot some pictures that could hardly be cut together because he kept changing the scenes from day to day. He directed *Touch of Evil* right after my picture and, though it did fairly well, it took almost ten months to cut! To me, he could have been the genius of the film business if he'd only had a little discipline.

Man in the Shadow was modestly budgeted at $600,000 and shot in black-and-white and CinemaScope, almost entirely on the Universal lot. Its story of a power-mad tyrant finally brought down by the outrage of the oppressed is loosely based on situations allegedly involving the notorious King Ranch in Texas. An elderly ranch worker comes to Sheriff Ben Sadler (Jeff Chandler) with a story that a young Mexican has been beaten to death by the ranch foreman and his assistant. Investigating, Sheriff Sadler finds false information, removed evidence, and closed doors that mean no help from the Golden Empire Ranch or the town. When his persistence results in a brutal chastisement witnessed by the reluctant townfolk, they finally come to his support, resulting in arrest for the rancher and his henchmen.

While the plot of *Man in the Shadow* is essentially melodrama, a concerted attempt was made to make the film as realistic as possible. The studio, writer, director, and cast seriously desired to make a film touching on the theme of racial injustice and oppression. The *New York Times* said that there may have been better westerns than

Man in the Shadow, "... but few, at least recently, as honest ... or as unpretentiously purposeful.... This ... production is not a big picture, nor a vividly dramatic one, for all Mr. Chandler's martyrdom. Just a good, blunt little one, ticking away with the steady matter-of-factness of an old-fashioned alarm clock. And sounding off just as reliably."[15]

The performances are quite good; Chandler's restrained, strong sheriff is a match for Welles' powerful rancher, and the co-stars and supporting players are all fine, with the possible exceptions of Joe Schneider as the murdered Mexican lad and Martin Garralaga as the old Mexican who witnessed the murder. There is nothing really wrong with their respective performances; rather, they seem miscast, as they do not look, and indeed are not, Mexican. This seems strange in a city with as many Mexicans as Los Angeles, though the probable reason is simply that there were no suitable Mexican actors already on contract with U-I, and the studio intended to use only the people they already had.

Man in the Shadow was released in November 1957 on the top half of a double bill co-featuring another Albert Zugsmith production, *The Female Animal.* Reviewers correctly noted that, "Jack Arnold has directed ... for full dramatic values...."[16] "*Man in the Shadow* is an interesting, rather offbeat melodrama ... considerably brightened by thoughtful casting.... Jack Arnold has directed for human element as well as suspense and excitement."[17]

Later that year Arnold left Universal-International for offers at MGM and Paramount (see Chapter 5). Upon his return to U-I in mid–1958 he was assigned to *Monster on the Campus,* one of U-I's more overtly exploitative "B" thrillers. It was produced by Joseph Gershenson, music director at U-I, responsible for fine music tracks on many of Arnold's pictures.

> Joseph Gershenson was a very fine man who wanted like crazy to be a producer. Universal finally gave him his chance with *Monster on the Campus* and I was assigned to direct. The science fiction craze was dying out and I really didn't want to do this kind of picture. But as a contract director I had little choice. I had to do it or risk being suspended. There were many problems with the script, but the studio liked it and wanted us to go right ahead with the picture. I tried very hard to do the best I could with it but we had a very tight schedule. If I had it to do all over again with more time and a little rewriting I could make it into a good picture. It's not one of my favorites.

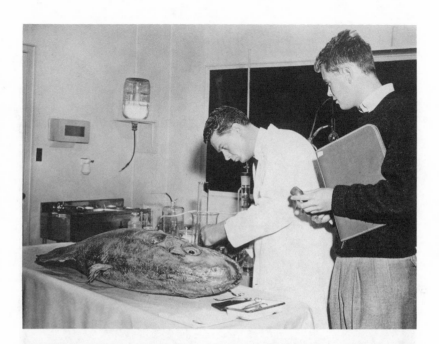

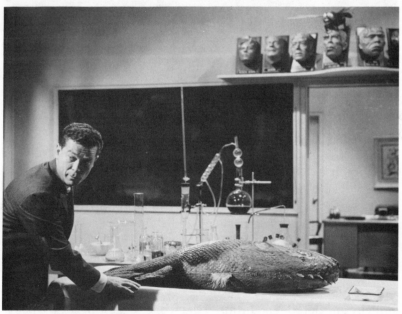

Monster on the Campus. *At top, Professor Donald Blake (Arthur Franz, left) and student Jimmy Flanders (Troy Donahue) examine a prehistoric coelacanth "preserved by atomic radiation." Below, Blake looks for a way to defend himself from a dive-bombing dragonfly (on bust in upper right-hand corner), which grew to monster proportions after drinking the coelacanth's blood.*

Stuntman Eddie Parker doubling for Arthur Franz as the prehistoric terror of Monster on the Campus. *The monster is carrying Joanna Moore, who is apparently unconscious but nevertheless manages to keep her legs nicely crossed.*

Monster on the Campus was U-I's response to the rising "teenage monster" trend of the late 1950s, and is a superior entry in that narrow sub-genre. The quality of the film actually seems a bit too good for such a farfetched premise. A science professor (Arthur Franz) has a coelacanth "preserved by atomic radiation" shipped to the college campus. Upon arrival, a police dog laps up a few drops of its blood and is temporarily transformed into a sabre-toothed wolf. The professor accidentally cuts his finger on the fish's teeth and blacks out, only to discover, upon awakening, that a pretty nurse has been brutally murdered. Footprints at the scene suggest those of a paleolithic sub-human. The professor begins to suspect that he is himself the killer after he sees a dragonfly, sipping coelacanth blood, transform into a giant prehistoric version of itself. A few drops of the blood accidentally drip into the professor's pipe; when he lights up he again blacks out. He comes to, and finds that a detective has been murdered. Convinced that he is indeed the killer, he retreats to a remote mountain cabin with a camera, tape recorder, and syringe of fish blood, in order to record his bizarre transformation for science. As he is turning into a monster, his worried fiancée (Joanna Moore) arrives, soon followed by the police. Knowing he is guilty of murder, the monster allows himself to be gunned down, and then transforms back into his regular self before our eyes. The story is essentialy a modern Dr. Jekyll with few surprises and even greater strain on our credulity.

Contemporary reviewers, however, didn't seem to mind a bit, and considered *Monster on the Campus* rather intellectual for a film of this type. The *Hollywood Reporter* went into some detail in its instructive review:

> Like most good horror stories, this one uses actual fact and current scientific theory as a springboard. About a year ago, the newspapers told of the catching, in the Indian Ocean, of a coelacanth, a species of fish whose evolution had been arrested millions of years ago at a point where its fins were on the point of turning into rudimentary legs. It had long been considered extinct. At about the same time, Russian scientists advanced the theory that mutations of living species were caused by atomic action and that the age of the great reptiles ended in the prehistoric past, because of solar explosions of great violence. Duncan's script combines this incident and hypothesis . . .[18]

Variety called *Monster on the Campus* ". . . expertly produced story of retrogression," and went on to state, "Its premise is logically developed without any great strain on the imagination, acting is convincing and there's a general professional air about the unfoldment. Film is a good entry for its particular exploitation market. . . . Jack Arnold's direction . . . builds constant suspense and provides a sock climax."[19]

Monster on the Campus is not nearly as bad as would appear from the title, and got more than it deserved from director Jack Arnold. In a recent assessment Ed Naha described the film as a ". . . charming excursion into brainless fluff. Could only have been made in the fifties."[20] It also has the distinction of being Troy Donahue's first film. *Monster on the Campus* is televised with reasonable regularity, and is more entertaining than one would suspect.

Arnold next co-produced and directed an Audie Murphy

western, the kind of picture usually regarded as ordinary in the extreme. It may be recalled that ". . . it was Murphy, along with Joel
McCrea and Randolph Scott, who held together the last vestiges of
the B-western during the fifties and sixties. In fact, Audie was the last
authentic hero of the double-bill western picture."[21] According to
the trade reviews, *No Name on the Bullet* was strictly intended for the
bottom half of the double bill. However, even the most understanding and sympathetic reviewers entirely missed the film's most interesting qualities. It is decidedly not an action melodrama, but
rather a highly refined, even philosophical drama examining the
nature of good and evil and the emptiness of merely conventional
morality.

The central question of the drama is under what conditions, if
any, man has the right to the power of life and death over his fellows.
The screenplay by Gene L. Coon *(Man in the Shadow)*, based on a
Howard Amaker story, develops the many implications of this question through a thoughtful interplay of personalities.

Audie Murphy plays John Gant, a notorious hired killer who has
escaped the law because he always goads his victim into drawing
first. His mere presence in town means that someone is marked for
death; those with something to hide fear he is out to kill them. Dr.
Luke Canfield (Charles Drake), town physician, introduces himself
to Gant and hopes to persuade him of the immortality of killing or
at least to get Gant to leave town. He discovers to his surprise that
Gant is a quiet, intelligent, and highly cultured man, if somewhat
melancholic. Over a game of chess the doctor discovers Gant to be
disarmingly articulate on questions of morality. If anything, Gant appears less dogmatic and more reasonable than the doctor. Gant poses
the following hypothetical question: If, on the one hand, a criminal
eludes justice but a man like Gant puts a permanent end to his mis-
deeds, while, on the other hand, a doctor heals such a man so that
he may continue his rapacity against the innocent — who, the gunman
or the doctor, is morally culpable? The doctor is nonplussed. Gant
further suggests that he, too, is a kind of healer, though of social ills,
and he reminds the doctor that "everybody dies."

John Gant's presence has caused guilty citizens of the town to
self-destruct. A banker kills himself, others shoot each other, another
flees town. Gant's intended victim, however, is a tubercular former
judge (Edgar Stehli), marked for death for having been part of a conspiracy involving a mayor and a governor. As he is about to die

No Name on the Bullet. *At top, Doctor Luke Canfield (Charles Drake) attends one of gunman John Gant's victims. Below, philosophical gunman Gant (Audie Murphy) defends himself by disarming Canfield in the final reel.*

anyway, the judge intends to force Gant to draw first—so that he will hang. The judge's unmarried daughter (Joan Evans), determined to stop this, confronts Gant in his hotel room, and attempts to shoot him with a derringer. She reveals her father's intention to get Gant to shoot first. Gant, in a rare show of anger, disarms her and tears a piece off her bodice. We are left to speculate what other liberties he may have taken, as we find ourselves at the judge's ranch. The judge tells Gant he won't defend himself and says that Gant is going to hang. Gant then shows the piece of bodice to him, insinuating that he had forced himself on the judge's daughter. The judge loses control, struggles out of his wheelchair, and attempts to shoot Gant. Gant, with quiet self-assurance, walks out of the house toward his horse. The judge, highly agitated, gets as far as the front porch, where he tries to take aim at Gant. As he raises the shotgun he collapses of a fatal heart attack; the firearm goes off harmlessly. Gant instinctively draws and turns, but instantly sees what has happened.

Meanwhile the doctor has found the judge's daughter, unmolested, and has hurried with the sheriff to the judge's house, arriving just as Gant is holstering his gun. Presuming that Gant has killed the old man, the doctor hurls a blacksmith's hammer at him, shattering his shooting arm. The sheriff arrives at the judge's side, and in a moment it is evident that Gant has killed no one. Gant stoically refuses an offer of medical aid. He says to the doctor, "A lot of men would like to kill John Gant, but it took a healer with a hammer to make it easy for them." As he rides away he tries to ease the doctor's conscience by telling him that "all things come to a finish."

The screenplay is unusually well written and thoughtful. The healer is quick to blame Gant for the deaths of men who destroyed themselves because of their own guilt. The judge, a man who once held the power of life or death in sentencing, is himself guilty of some great and unnamed crime that had escaped justice. His presumably pure and virginal daughter is willing to go beyond the law and kill for the sake of her own selfish attachment to her father. Even the audience is invited to presume that Gant is about to molest her when he tears the piece from her dress. But Gant is himself innocent, almost a metaphysical force that catalyzes the evil inherent in others. He is the only completely honest and integrated being in the story. The final irony is that the healer deliberately commits an injury that will result in the death of an innocent man. His attachment to dogmatic morality results in injustice and death.

Audie Murphy was a delicate, sensitive little man. Considering his background and war experiences, the character of John Gant seems particularly appropriate for him. Credit must be given to Jack Arnold for understanding both the delicacy of the script and actor; a less sensitive director could have ruined the film. Arnold had the intelligence to direct unobtrusively, backing away almost to the point of neutrality, thereby not overwhelming his material. He also succeeds in establishing a foreboding atmosphere that supports the generally low-key happenings. The deliberate, even cadence with which the story unfolds maintains our interest without resorting to obvious tricks, and Arnold made everybody, especially Mr. Murphy, look good.

No Name on the Bullet was released in February, 1959, served its purpose as a bottom-bill western, and was promptly forgotten. This is unfortunate, as the intelligent script, restrained performances, and smooth direction leave the film relatively undated; certainly its meaning is as relevant as ever. It was the last film Jack Arnold made as a contract director for Universal-International.

Arnold looks back with pleasure on his days as a contract director at Universal.

It was exciting. We didn't make a fortune, but we had a good time. MGM was considered the Tiffany of studios, and we were the May Company. MGM had Clark Gable and Liz Taylor. Next came Warners with Bogart, Bacall, and Edward G. Robinson. We had Tony Curtis, Jeff Chandler, Rock Hudson, and Janet Leigh. Fritz Lang was gone and the young contract directors were Blake Edwards, Joe Pevney, and me. It was like a college campus — and we had great parties!

5
Spaced Kids and
Space Children

There were changes taking place at Universal-International in the late 1950s; Edward Muhl, vice president in charge of production, came under the control of general sales manager Alfred Daff, and things were never quite the same. "That's when I left," said producer Albert Zugsmith. "I wouldn't have left if Eddie Muhl could have run the show."[1] Mr. Zugsmith's agent, Charles Feldman, got him a deal with Metro-Goldwyn-Mayer, and production began on what is perhaps the greatest teen exploitation flick of all time, *High School Confidential!*

Jack Arnold was not impressed by the choice of subject matter, but was happy to have the opportunity to direct at MGM. "For one thing, they paid better," he says. To this day Jack affects a certain indifference to *High School Confidential!*, perhaps due in part to his attitude toward its producer. Yet there can be little doubt that it was Jack Arnold's directorial contribution that pulled the film together, and set it above the others of the "wild youth" genre.

Youth movie historian Richard Staeling describes the emergence of this genre, and offers an appreciation of *High School Confidential!*:

> Less than a year after the debut of rock musicals and mild youth melodramas, a third genre appeared, most likely as a backlash reaction to such adolescent fluff. Packed with action, sex, drugs, and parental hypocrisy, the wild youth films were sensationalism with no apologies; the *National Enquirer* of teen movies.
> Of the twenty-five to thirty films of this sort, none rises from

Love among the hopheads: Diane Jergens and Russ Tamblyn in Arnold's High School Confidential!

the depths showing as much class as . . . *High School Confidential!*
. . . it followed the pattern set by American-International and
Allied Artists releases of 1957/1958, surpassing them in every
respect. . . . Not enough can be said to recommend this farfetched tale of high schoolers and the evil weed . . . a classic in
the genre.[2]

High School Confidential! has been an unqualified success since its release in June of 1958. Made quickly for a mere $517,000, it reputedly grossed about $8,000,000 before its revival in the mid–1970s. Producer Zugsmith notes that "it broke the all-time house record at Loew's State in New York City when it was first released. Its world premiere was in Atlantic City, N.J.—at the old Apollo tryout house on the boardwalk—and it broke the house record there, too. The initial reaction to it was sensational. Right off, everybody claimed I was some kind of a dope-user who was out of his head."[3]

The reason one might have thought this of Mr. Zugsmith is that, while the film purports to have a straight anti-drug message, the young drug addicts are portrayed sympathetically and are hip and charismatic. And while the film opens with an absurdly straight-faced warning by Dr. Stuart Knox ("While parents sleep, their children are being turned into addicts."), Arnold cuts directly to Jerry Lee Lewis pounding out explosive rock and roll for a mob of dance-frenzied teens. From that moment on, the tension between the film's supposed anti-drug message and the cinematic subversion of that message begins to build.

Mr. Zugsmith insists that *High School Confidential!* is a serious film, a "well-researched, realistic study of marijuana. . . . We felt that the subject of pot should be analyzed and handled in a realistic manner and that we should not take sides on it . . . also, we wanted to make a chronicle of the exact time." He further states that in order to assure "maximum authenticity," he interviewed narcotics officers, and frequented Venice coffee houses and private pot parties—to talk to the teenagers using marijuana. "I wanted to get how the kids really felt about pot; to find out what happened to kids who used it," he says.[4]

Anyone who has seen *High School Confidential!* might wonder if Mr. Zugsmith was talking about another picture of the same name. He doubtless had a great deal to do with the choice of subject, casting of Mamie Van Doren, and the exploitation campaign, but it is obvious that he delegated the actual making of the film to a considerable degree, deferring to the expertise of his director. Arnold says, "Zugsmith wanted an out-and-out exploitation picture, a straight, preachy, message film—and if I could put nudity in it that would be great! I got along very well with Zugsmith. I just didn't agree with him on everything, but he didn't insist, which was a pleasure. If he didn't like what I did I would just say, 'Well, I like it,' and he'd leave me alone."

High School Confidential! *At top, Jerry Lee Lewis and his band perform "Boppin' at the High School Hop" in the opening reel. At bottom, Tony (Russ Tamblyn), having stolen his switchblade back from the principal, cleans his nails with it while relaxing at the principal's desk.*

High School Confidential! *At top, Tony (Russ Tamblyn) with his "Aunt" Gwen (Mamie Van Doren), who seems to be offering him more than a glass of milk. At bottom, head dope pusher Mr. "A" (Jackie Coogan, center) and his henchman, Bix (Ray Anthony, left), offer Tony a shot of "the hard stuff."*

High School Confidential! is primarily the creation of the writer, the director and the cast. However, no one who has seen the film can possibly imagine that these people were all taking the picture seriously. This tongue-in-cheek quality is what makes the film so entertaining; it is self-consciously lurid in a restrained and stylized way, yet never lapses into bad taste.

> I never intended to kid the film, I just set out to tell the story. The picture's "message" wasn't all that profound, and if I'd done a straight, preachy, drugs-are-terrible movie, who would have come? I had to put an edge on it. It wasn't exactly comedy; I just pushed parts of the story until they were bigger than life. I was in a crazy mood, but I'd be lying if I said I made it deliberately tongue-in-cheek. Besides, I didn't know anything about dope; I had to assume the script was right. Now I know it wasn't, and that the business about marijuana leading to heroin is silly.

The script, by Lewis Meltzer and Robert Blees *(The Glass Web)*, is utterly preposterous from beginning to end. Unknown to fellow students at Santa Bello High School—and to the audience for much of the film—Tony Baker (Russ Tamblyn) is in reality an undercover narcotics agent when he registers as a transfer student from Chicago. His brash manner and hipster talk soon ingratiate him with the worst element and he succeeds in making contact with a drug pusher (John Drew Barrymore). Tony lives at the home of his aunt (Mamie Van Doren), who repeatedly attempts to ambush him from behind a very tight sweater. Tony shows more interest in his English teacher (Jan Sterling) and a pretty student (Diane Jergens), who is "hooked" on marijuana. In an attempt to "score" the "hard stuff," Tony is introduced to Mr. "A" (Jackie Coogan), who plays jazz in a sort of combination dope-den/malt shop. Tony makes his "bust" with the help of judo and the police, and the pretty hophead kicks the stuff after some tender counseling from the English teacher.

High School Confidential! abounds in events and situations that are highly improbable, if not downright bizarre. The title sequence features Jerry Lee Lewis and band performing "Boppin' at the High School Hop"[5] on the back of a flatbed truck passing slowly through the schoolyard; scores of dancing kids follow him as if he were the Pied Piper. We are supposed to believe, according to a banner on the truck, that Jerry sells used records off this truck, and is singing just to drum up a little business. There is also the very strange, almost incestuous, relation between Tony and his "aunt." The script never bothers to clear up the mystery of whether Mamie actually is his aunt or whether she is another police plant who takes her work too seriously. It is obvious that the writer and director had no difficulty with this; the mere presence of Miss Van Doren was apparently sufficient justification for any possible ambiguity.

Equally fantastic is Jackie Coogan's characterization of Mr. "A." Is it really possible that this smiling owner of the jazz club/malt shop/dope den actually works for the Mafia and sells teenage girls who have graduated to the "hard stuff" into prostitution? It is amusing to note that in the scene where Tony meets with Mr. "A" in his secret backroom office to discuss a heroin deal, Jackie Coogan affects a pair of black sunglasses; apparently he wears them only when he is selling dope in order to give himself a proper air of menace.

Earlier, when Tony is in the principal's office, his switchblade is confiscated. Not long afterwards he is threatened by some toughs in the locker room and — as if by magic — produces his switchblade. Just as the audience begins to wonder where the knife came from, Tony says, "I lost one of these in the principal's office, I don't want to lose another one in your belly." This would be a clumsy bit of exposition if the writer wasn't laughing up his sleeve.

There is a very funny scene in which a narcotics commissioner explains the evils of marijuana to the high school teachers and principal. There is a big close-up where he says, totally deadpan, "You will notice that there is a great difference in appearance between marijuana and an ordinary cigarette." The art direction adds a good touch to this scene; as the commissioner makes a fool of himself with an overdrawn sermon on the evils of marijuana, we see on the wall behind him a framed photograph of the Capitol Building in Washington, D.C., and another of a row of little men, perhaps a military regiment. It approaches satire.

We may compare this scene to another in which a beatnik poetess (Phillipa Fallon) recites to jazz accompaniment an articulate manifesto of zen-psychedelic hedonism:

My old man was a bread-stasher all his life;
He never got fat.
He wound up with a used car, a seventeen inch screen,
And arthritis.

Tomorrow is a drag, man.
Tomorrow is a king-size bust.

They cried, "Put down pot,
Don't think a lot."
For what?
Time, how much, and what to do with it.
Sleep, man, and you might wake up
Digging the whole human race
Giving itself three days to get out.
Tomorrow is a drag, Pops.
The future is a flake.

* * * *

Cool a fast short,
Swing with a gassy chick,
Turn on to a thousand joys.
Smile on what happened
Or check what's going to happen,
You'll miss what's happening.
Turn your eyes inside
And dig the vacuum.
Tomorrow, drag.[6]

Who can doubt that Miss Fallon's very hip recitation and exhortation to "turn on" had a much greater influence on the attitudes of a young audience than the silly scarestories of the narcotics commissioner?

The epilogue, however, is the dead giveaway. A voice-over (Paul Frees doing his authoritarian announcer voice) tells us how justice has triumphed in this case but that we must be ever vigilant of the insidious marijuana menace, etc. This is over a shot of Russ Tamblyn driving in his Lincoln convertible, two blondes by his side (Jan Sterling and Diane Jergens), while Mamie Van Doren lies sprawled on the back seat passionately embracing her "husband" (who has returned, as the voice-over informs us). Someone is pulling our leg.

High School Confidential! is deliberately and stylishly ludicrous, lampooning the anti-marijuana ideologues while glamorizing the erstwhile dopers. This latter aspect did not escape the notice of the federal narcotics people who sensed that the film was a dope, rock-and-roll, sex, and fast-car escapist fantasy for teens. "Harry Anslinger, who was the head federal narc at the time, demanded we depict the bad effects of marijuana," explains producer Zugsmith. "Otherwise, they weren't going to allow the film to be shown at all. The legal department of MGM got a directive from Anslinger . . . the

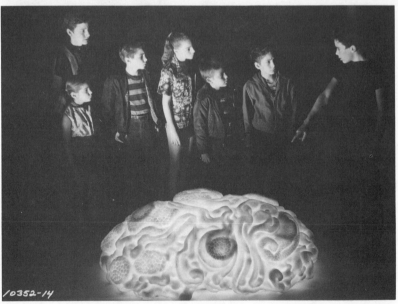

The Space Children. At top, young Bud Brewster (Michel Ray) realizes the alien voice is coming to him telepathically. Below, the weird brain-like extra-terrestrial gives Bud and the gang orders to sabotage the experimental missile.

Bud (Michel Ray, in center of children's group) and the other kids shield the space creature (the brainlike blob behind them) until it can evanesce back whence it came in the final reel of The Space Children.

narcotics people raised too much hell. So the statements that had to be made were made. But only because they *had* to be made."[7]

However, the anti-marijuana message in *High School Confidential!* in no way impairs the film's primary purpose as escapist fantasy. Because it *is* fantasy, and not a realistic chronicle of the times, it is still a wildly entertaining film, expertly crafted by artists that had fun doing it. It remains one of the best-loved and most enjoyable cult films of all time.

William Alland was another producer who left U-I in late 1957. Signing with Paramount, he began production of two science-fiction programmers intended to be released as a double bill, *The Space Children* and *The Colossus of New York*. The idea was to release them together so that both would not be sold off cheaply as bottom bill pictures. *The Colossus of New York* is a kiddie matinée Frankenstein; a scientist's brain is transplanted into a huge robot, who is then befriended by the scientist's son. Directed by Eugene Lourie, *Colossus* has a certain naive charm, but is nothing really special. *The Space*

Children, on the other hand, is a very serious little picture dealing with mankind's capacity for self-destruction and renewal; Jack Arnold was asked to direct.

Both pictures were inexpensive, budgeted at less than half of what was typically spent on U-I's science fiction pictures. "My interest," said Alland in a contemporary interview,

> . . . is in the challenge of trying to make a good, entertaining picture at a cost geared to guaranteed audience potential. That is, $600,000 gross domestic and, if we send it overseas, $150,000 or $200,000 more. This is a gross you can count on.
>
> At U-I in '52 $1,000,000 was considered the certain gross of any picture, no matter how bad. So if it was made for $500,000, the operation was considered to be on a safe basis. Today, with the gross down to $600,000, we must spend no more than $300,000 to be sure of breaking even. Now that same $300,000 at a major studio would mean only $175,000 at an independent. But I say the picture you can turn out at a major is, dollar for dollar, much better in quality.[8]

The Space Children may be a small film, but it is elegant. The story, performances, effects and direction fuse to create a little film that is beautiful and unique. Moreover, its message to children and adults is as timely and relevant now as when the film was made.

The story centers around a group of children living with their parents in a cliffside trailer park on the California coast. The parents are technicians, working on a secret "six-stage rocket" armed with a nuclear satellite that could instantly destroy any city in the world. The children notice a strange beam of light coming down from the sky and follow it to a cave where they discover a gelatinous, glowing, brain-like creature that *thinks* to them. Linking minds with the creature, the children use telekinesis to spoil the launch, resulting in the rocket's destruction. The alien being leaves the way it came, and the children inform their parents that this has happened all over the world, and that all nuclear weapons have been destroyed. As one of the mothers remarks, "The world has been given a second chance." The film ends with a biblical quotation: "Yea, I say unto you, except ye become as little children, ye shall not enter into the kingdom of heaven."

Ideologically, the film might be considered controversial even today, as one scientist (Jackie Coogan) suggests the satellite be used as a first-strike weapon to annihilate the Russians, and the children perform acts of civil disobedience in order to destroy the nuclear weapons. The film strongly suggests that only children have the sense to do this; the adults are portrayed as hopelessly corrupted by divisive and destructive ideologies. There is a degree of truth present here that is uncommon in most films of its genre. It is also subtly suggested that the alien may be some kind of divine emissary.

The Space Children is directed in a lean, economical style. Long shots are on location; dialogue close-ups are composed before a process screen. The only studio sets of any consequence are a small corner of the trailer park and the grotto where the alien is hiding. Camera movement is fluid, and is especially effective tracking the children through the alien's grotto. The scenes on the beach are very atmospheric, reminiscent of the desert in *It Came from Outer Space*. Casting and performances are good, with Michel Ray, the lad who leads the other children, the easy standout. Much of his performance is without dialogue, his facial expressions alone revealing the thoughts transmitted to him by the alien. Russell Johnson is memorable as a drunken father driven to madness and death when he is stopped from striking his step-son by the alien's psychic power.

Arnold is fond of *The Space Children*, and enjoyed working with his young cast. "I like the film very much. I had a lot of fun working with those kids—when I could keep them away from their stage mothers. It was all make-believe for them, and they understood exactly what I wanted with no trouble at all. They were really into the whole experience and had no hang-ups whatsoever."

The Space Children is seldom seen today and seems never to have been syndicated to television. Perhaps it was suppressed for its anti-authority and anti-nuclear message. One can well imagine a conservative syndication or programming executive simply letting the film slip silently into oblivion. It is certainly an excellent candidate for revival today. The story is of contemporary relevance, while the dress and mannerisms of the characters seem more archetypically American than many a recent portrayal of similar types. An interesting and thoughtful film for adults, it is also an excellent children's film and might have a place in schools and libraries.

6
The Mouse That Roared

In the summer of 1958, Jack Arnold was contacted by his friend Julius Epstein, Oscar winning co-author of *Casablanca;* it seemed that Carl Foreman was looking for a "fresh talent" to direct a comedy feature in England. The project had begun when Columbia publicist Walter Shenson bought the motion picture rights to *The Mouse That Roared,* a novel by Leonard Wibberly serialized in *The Saturday Evening Post.* Mr. Shenson had been trying for about five years to get the story produced before he presented it to Carl Foreman. Mr. Foreman's company, High Road Productions, had just finished *The Key,* and was engaged in pre-production on *The Guns of Navarone.* Something was needed to charge office expenses to, and an inexpensive comedy like *The Mouse* was perfect. A deal was struck, and production got under way.

The story of *The Mouse That Roared* is based on the old joke about a tiny country purposely losing a war with the United States in order to reap the benefits of reconstruction aid; to this was added satirical comment on the arms race and the nuclear threat in particular. The Duchy of Grand Fenwick, smallest country in the world, relies for its existence on the export of their local wine. When a cheaper, California imitation brings Grand Fenwick's economy to the point of collapse, the Prime Minister (Peter Sellers) suggests the plan of losing a war with America, and reaping the benefits: "The Americans always rush to the aid of the people they defeat. . . . They pour money into the country of their former enemies and do anything to save the people they've beaten." The Prime Minister and Duchess Gloriana (also Peter Sellers) send hereditary Field Marshal Tully Bascombe (Sellers *again*) and twenty chain-mail clad warriors to

Top: *Jack Arnold's wife, Betty (left), chats between takes with actress Jean Seberg (center) and Mrs. Walter Shenson, the producer's wife, on the set of* The Mouse That Roared. *Bottom:* Hereditary Field Marshal Tully Bascombe *(Peter Sellers) seems to be having a bit of trouble with his bow in this great sight gag from* The Mouse That Roared.

invade the United States. They arrive to find New York apparently deserted; actually, there is a citywide air raid drill (due to new fears generated by America's development of the portable Q-bomb, the most destructive weapon in the world). Tully and his men wander about searching for someone to surrender to, but cause panic among civil defense workers, who think they are men from Mars. In the confusion, Tully accidentally captures the Q-bomb, its inventor, his daughter, a general, and four of New York's "finest." They return to Grand Fenwick to the great consternation of the Prime Minister, but wise Duchess Gloriana uses her possession of the bomb to get a million-dollar loan from the U.S. Treasury, the California wine taken off the market, and nuclear disarmament for the world. Tully Bascombe is promoted to Prime Minister, and marries the inventor's daughter (Jean Seberg).

The Mouse That Roared is a very funny film; it addresses serious subjects in a light way. The portrayal of the American general and foreign diplomats is pointedly satirical, but not overly offensive. For example, a message from Moscow reads, "Of course we invented the Q-bomb twenty years ago, but the working people of this great democracy are greatly interested in seeing that your Q-bomb does not fall into the hands of the capitalist war-mongering hyenas," while the British Prime Minister claims that the Duchy is ". . . closely and vitally linked with Britain—almost a member of the Commonwealth." In one scene a diverse group of diplomats from major powers waits outside the gates of the castle. To pass time they play a game together, a board game like "Monopoly." The game, however, is called "Diplomacy," and has the players trading territories, ruining economies, etc. in order to win. They appear to be having great fun.

Toward the end of the film the bomb's inventor drops it, but it doesn't go off. He asks the bomb, "Are you a dud?" One is tempted to read into his pained expression the realization that nuclear weapons are finally useless in terms of improving the human condition.

The seriousness of the arms race is brought out in a wonderful scene in which the bomb has begun making hideous noises, as if it is about to go off. The football-like bomb is accidentally tossed into a crowd of diplomats; each one wanted to get the bomb for his own country, but none of them wants the bomb himself. The terrified diplomats toss the bomb to each other in a manner resembling a football

The Mouse That Roared. Top: *Finding an empty city when he arrives in New York during an air raid drill, Hereditary Field Marshal Tully Bascombe (Peter Sellers) and his soldiers consult their* Thomas Cook's Guide. *Bottom: The Army of Grand Fenwick, led by Tully Bascombe (Sellers), ambushes a jeep in Central Park capturing General Snippet (MacDonald Parke, in front passenger's seat of Jeep) and four New York City policemen on a tour of inspection during the air raid drill.*

game. The whole scene takes on the character of a Mack Sennett chase. Suddenly, when the tension is at its highest, there is a cut to an extreme long shot of a nuclear explosion. The audience is aghast. The game of nuclear armament goes on every day among the world's diplomats, yet we act as if the bombs will never really go off. Fortunately, in the film, an announcer's voice comes over the shot of the mushroom cloud, assuring us that the film is not over, but that the producers only wished to give the audience an idea of what *might* happen. It is a shocking, but very funny scene. *The Mouse That Roared* may be comedy, but Arnold's personal outrage at the state of the world gives it a tense, subtextual urgency.

> It was a way of making a social comment I felt was important . . . the most effective way to make a social comment is to do it by satire and comedy. . . . Those who were sophisticated enough to get the meanings we were putting into the film got it, and those who enjoyed the slapstick comedy—visual comedy, enjoyed that aspect of the film. If you're going to say something that means something and has a message, I think you should do it satirically and do it in a way that audiences will get it even though they're not aware of it, that they're getting it. . . . You have to do it through comedy, a satirical, soft touch. A whole spectrum of audiences have found *Mouse* enjoyable . . . this was proven by its reception.

The Mouse That Roared has been a very successful film, grossing about $50,000,000 in all markets to date. However, not everyone immediately recognized the film's potential. As the director recalls,

> *The Mouse That Roared* was very strange in the making—and in the finishing. Walter and I laughed a lot at the dailies in London, but Carl Foreman and Whiteman, head of Columbia in Europe, weren't laughing. They thought it was a disaster. It was so discouraging I quit going to dailies and asked Walter to watch them for me and see if they were any good.
>
> When the film was completed, they didn't know what they had. As a matter of fact when we previewed the finished film (we did it in two theatres in New York—at the Trans-Lux Theatre, which was kind of an arthouse, sophisticated audience, and at Loew's 84th Street, which was kind of proletariat) it went so well—they laughed so hard in both houses—that Foreman immediately had all the prints recalled, changed "High Road presents" to "Carl Foreman presents" and opened it at the prestigious Guild Theater in New York. It went so well at the

People's Representative Benter (Leo McKern, left) and Prime Minister Montjoy (Peter Sellers) plot escape from Grand Fenwick with Helen (Jean Seberg). This was the first scene shot in The Mouse That Roared; *according to Arnold, Jean Seberg became flustered, and after 25 takes, the scene was reshot on another day.*

preview, they didn't know what they had until they saw an audience reaction. Being the director of the film, I knew what we had, and I thought it would be a successful film. I didn't think it would be as successful as it was because we made it for only $450,000, which wasn't a lot of money even in those days.

Mouse is my favorite film because I was able to make use of what I proudly call my sense of humor. . . . I had definite opinions. . . . I thought I expressed them in that film in a way that is acceptable to a mass audience. I'm anti-war . . . and I think what governments do—I'll say it kindly—is childish. I thought we should show the idiocy of what we adults make of our government, besides having a lot of fun doing it, making people laugh and maybe think a little bit, too. So, not only because it's essentially satirical and gave full reign to whatever comedic talents I may have, it also was a vehicle for me to express my own opinion.

And luckily there was no pressure on me from anybody, except to make a good film from Walter Shenson who was the line producer and who was in complete agreement with what I wanted to do, so he was a help, no hindrance. We cast the best actors we could find. In those days in England, we could cast anybody, we didn't have to pay a lot of money for them. So we made a very good film, I thought. I was very proud of it.

The producers left me alone because (1) they didn't think it meant anything, (2) they were just writing it off for expenses anyway. So I had no pressure on me at all. I'm used to shooting quickly and the time was no problem. . . . I cast it with the best actors I could find in England . . . they certainly know how to play this kind of satire. The only problem I had at the time was that Columbia insisted that I use Jean Seberg. They wanted somebody with a recognizable name. There was no one else in the film that anyone had ever heard of in the States. No one had ever heard of Peter Sellers. He was just a character actor, except for the Goon Show on radio and the West End. This is the first movie that made him a star.[1] Jean had just done *Saint Joan* and *Bonjour Tristesse* for Otto Preminger and was at least a name someone knew. She was a very lovely girl, but she'd come fresh from her indoctrination by Preminger into film acting. Preminger was a screamer and a yeller. He waited until he got her into hysterics, then he'd turn the camera on. I don't yell or scream and this was a new experience for her. Sometimes it took to take twenty to get it but we got it. The first scene we did was in her room in the castle in Grand Fenwick where Sellers and the other man who's supposed to be the working man's representative are plotting an escape. I said, "Jean, in this scene you walk over here and say your line to Peter, your attitude is obvious." When she came to her line she took a step forward, said her line, and stepped back again. I looked at her and said, "Let's try that again." She did the same thing that second time! Peter glared at me as if to say, "What the hell is this?" I took her aside privately, as I didn't want to embarrass her. I said, "Jean, don't take a step forward, say your line, and then step back. Just stay where you are." She said "Gee, was I doing that? I wasn't conscious of it." I said, "Well, *be* conscious of it. Don't do it." She then became so conscious of it she didn't know what she was saying. By take twenty-five Peter didn't know what he was saying either. He was just spouting gibberish. I could see that he was really getting crazy. I said "Alright, let's forget this scene. We'll do it tomorrow. Just work on it." I moved on to another sequence and eventually worked things out with Jean. She went on to become quite a good actress. Peter was a marvelous improvisational actor, brilliant if you got him on the

Opposite: *From* The Mouse That Roared. *At top, Tully and Will (Peter Sellers and William Hartnell) stumble across the laboratory of Dr. Kokintz and accidentally capture the ultimate weapon — the football-shaped Q-bomb. At bottom, kidnapped by the Army of Grand Fenwick, General Snippet (MacDonald Parke) is forced to carry the captured Q-bomb, while Dr. Kokintz's daughter, Helen (Jean Seberg), looks on.*

first take. The second take would be good, but after the third take
he could be really awful. If he had to repeat the same words too
many times they became meaningless. But it was such a joy to
work with Peter because he was such an inspired actor. Sometimes he would literally knock me off my feet. I'd fall down con-
vulsed with laughter!

I didn't have any studio pressures. The only thing I did do
was I didn't tell Columbia I was going to fool around with their
logo. . . . I didn't ask them for permission, I just shot it. The picture opens with the logo, the Statue of Liberty, the old Columbia
symbol, and suddenly she lifts her skirt and screams and runs off
with the electric bulb hanging and a little mouse on the pedestal.
I did that without asking permission because I knew if I asked
them they wouldn't let me do it. . . . It's sacred, you don't fool
around with their logo. But they laughed so hard at the theatre,
before the picture even began, when they previewed the film.
And of course Carl Foreman and Walter Shenson were in on it
and they loved it. So we said we won't tell them until we preview
it, you see. The audience laughed so hard, without even the story
beginning, just at the logo, that we were home free. . . . It set the
tone for the whole film. . . . Of course they (Columbia) didn't
touch it after that. No alterations were made. . . . It was Carl's and
Walter's and my cut. . . . We jointly did what editing we thought
we had to do, but we didn't touch it after the first showing.

They laughed so hard in those theatres that you could hardly
hear the dialogue. There were lines around the block. It got big
critical acclaim that brought a lot of good word-of-mouth about
the film. For a film to stay in one theatre (New York's Guild
Theatre) for two years is an achievement. It stayed for a year in
Paris in one theatre. Here in Los Angeles — it was unheard of — a
year at the Music Hall Theater in Beverly Hills. But it played, for
the first year or two, only in art theatres, then it went into general
release.

It was a little before its time. . . . The basic premise . . . plot
. . . thrust of the film is as pertinent today as it was in the late
fifties when we made it, even more so, perhaps. So, it hasn't been
hurt by time, it may have been aided by time. My personal opinion
is that it would have been a much larger success if it had been
made and released ten years later. . . . It would have gotten a
much wider audience than it did in art houses because they're
small houses and you can only do so much business in them. . . .
They filled them up, they did tremendous business but the houses
were small, and they were only in key cities, they weren't all over
the country. They were in New York, Chicago, Los Angeles and
maybe one or two other cities. . . . There were twenty-five or
thirty, maybe fifty, where the Ealing comedies played; they never
did get a general release.

The Mouse That Roared. Top: *The Captain (Stuart Sanders, right) and Second Officer (Ken Stanley) of* HMS *Queen Elizabeth try to ward off an attack by the Army of Grand Fenwick. This scene was added after Arnold's crew managed to shoot some serendipitous footage of the actual* Queen Elizabeth *while filming in Southampton.* Bottom: *The victorious Army of Grand Fenwick returns—with the Q-bomb.*

Tully fears Dr. Kokintz's sneeze may set off the Q-bomb. Left to right: Jean Seberg, David Kossoff, Peter Sellers.

The Mouse That Roared was an enjoyable creative challenge for Jack Arnold. He was given freedom and support by personalities whose own ideas he respected. This creative collaboration of Jack Arnold, Walter Shenson, and Carl Foreman helped every step of the production. It began with the screenplay by Roger MacDougall and Stanley Mann; Carl Foreman and Walter Shenson did some rewriting, and Arnold did some work on the shooting script:

> We changed the essence a little bit, I think for the better. . . . The original story is not what we made into a film. In the original story the queen was a young woman and there was a romance between the queen and Tully. I felt that the romance should be with the daughter of the scientist. She was *very* American, true blood real *American*. . . . I wanted that General to be that way, too.

This creative atmosphere made it possible for Arnold to take advantage of opportunities to improvise:

> There was a lot of improvisation that went on while making the film that came out rather well. . . . Accidentally, when I was in

Southampton shooting the little tugboat (doubling Southampton for Marseilles) . . . I saw the *Queen Elizabeth* coming in to Southampton. I was on the cameraboat and . . . over the radio I told the captain of the tug to get as close to the *Queen Elizabeth* as she could get, and tell all the boys to shoot arrows at her. I had three cameras on the boat itself . . . and we got a sensational little sequence.

Afterwards, in the studio, a section of HMS *Queen Elizabeth's* bridge was duplicated, and some additional dialogue written for the ship's captain and first mate. When this was cut together with the shots of the actual ship, a funny sequence emerged without the slightest hint of its improvisational origin. In addition, the appearance of the HMS *Queen Elizabeth* gives more scope and production value to the film.

The Grand Duchy itself rose for a time as a facade and court built on a great lawn on the back lot of Shepperton Studios, London. The surrounding countryside, near Maidenhead, doubled for the forests of Fenwick, noticed first when we are introduced to Duchess Gloriana driving her antique touring car, and featured later during the mad chase for the bomb.

We shot that sequence at a very beautiful time of the year, it was early October. It was cold, but the leaves had turned, and the bracken was gold. The colors were . . . beautiful. . . . Those wonderful autumn colors in the countryside were so breathtaking and photographed so well. . . . I had a very good English crew that were just marvelous, the cameraman [John Wilcox] was excellent. And a lot of the stuff we shot in rain; England is not famous for its climate. You couldn't see it, but it was raining in the park sequence and a lot of that stuff in the woods was in rain. I just said shoot it wide open and let's go. Sometimes the color looks better when it is overcast.

For the invasion of New York City, Arnold used a location in downtown London, "London proper," that had been bombed out during the war, and rebuilt with glass and concrete highrises. An intersection of two streets was used, with the addition of American cars, signs, etc. After the soldiers arrive in New York harbor (actually Southampton) there is a beautiful and mysterious interlude composed of scenes of an empty New York City accompanied by eerie evocative music and soprano voice. Arnold created this sequence by flying to New York and shooting empty streets at dawn on a Sunday;

these shots were intercut with some stills, the final result being most atmospheric.

Arnold was able to include many little details that support the action and meaning of the film. For example, in the scene where Tully and his medieval warriors march off to war to the cheers of jubilant Fenwickian patriots, Arnold has the little Fenwickian boys line up behind the soldiers, imitating them with their high marching steps. It is a subtle commentary on the way in which innocent youth follows the folly of their leaders. Other examples of interesting and humorous details occur during the establishing shot of the courtyard and castle of Grand Fenwick. While the scene lasts only a moment, the discerning eye will see a lady shaking a rug out of a castle window, and a peasant herding his goats in the court. Arnold feels that such details are very important to a film:

> The fabric of a film is made up of details — if the details are correct, the whole picture will come out. Those little touches are very important. . . . Even if they go by quickly, you get it almost subliminally . . . all those little things that make up the feeling . . . of the film. I wanted to give this little Duchy a feeling of reality. . . . Here is this little country minding its own business, but in big trouble. . . .

It is interesting to note that the first part of the film is made in the manner of a documentary — a documentary on the history and present economic crisis of Grand Fenwick. This sequence recalls Arnold's early career as a documentarist, creating such films as *Chicken of Tomorrow*. Later, when Tully and his chain mail–clad soldiers are mistaken by panicked civil defense workers for invaders from Mars, the film takes on a deliberate science fiction quality, reminiscent of Arnold's years at U-I. The fact that the film is a comedy both recalls many fine comic moments in his previous, more serious films, and foreshadows the direction his career was about to take.

The Mouse That Roared had its U.S. release in October 1959 and got excellent critical notices. The *New York Times* called it a "rambunctious satiric comedy . . ." and continued, "We've got to hand it to Roger MacDougall and Stanley Mann, who wrote the script; to Jack Arnold, who directed, and to all the people who play in this lively jape. They whip up a lot of cheerful nonsense that makes wild fun of the awesome instruments of war and does so in terms of

social burlesque and sheer Mack Sennett farce."[2] Jack Arnold recalls
his reaction to this:

> The interesting part, for me anyway, was when the film opened
> in New York it got sensational reviews—but they gave credit to
> the British! One said, "When the British put their best effort into
> satire no one can top them." Even the *Motion Picture Herald* said,
> "Only the British could be so funny." Of course both Walter Shen-
> son and I are American. We had a little laugh at that. . . .
>   It did very, very well indeed, and, as I said, it is my favorite
> film for many reasons.

7
Ups and Downs
of a Working Director

The late 1950s saw the continued decline of feature production in Hollywood; the studios were increasingly employed in television production. By the early 1960s the program picture had almost entirely disappeared, or rather had migrated to television in the form of half-hour western, adventure, and comedy shows made on the same back lots by the same people who had formerly made the program pictures. It is not surprising, then, to find Jack Arnold turning increasingly to television for employment during this period. "We had to get into television," Arnold recalls, "because of the economy at the time. It was getting bad. Pictures weren't being made in the quantity that they had been. To stay alive one got into television. But having been brought up in the features, television was something of a step down. That's the way we used to think about it. I didn't want to become known as a television director."

Arnold did his first television work with Blake Edwards in the late 1950s. Like Arnold, Edwards had been a contract director at Universal-International. Edwards met the threat of low feature output by developing the successful television series *Mr. Lucky*, produced in 1959–60 with both men sharing production and directorial duties. Their partnership continued for the equally successful *Peter Gunn* series. In the following years Arnold went on to direct over 200 prime-time hours for all three networks including episodes of *Wagon Train, Perry Mason, Rawhide, Line-up, Kraft Theater, The Eleventh Hour, The Bob Hope Show, The Danny Thomas Hour, Gilligan's Island, It's About Time, Mod Squad,* and many others.

On the set of the Mr. Lucky television series at MGM. Top: Arnold (center) with series star John Vivyan (left) and series music composer Henry Mancini (right). Bottom: Jack Arnold with Gloria Swanson.

While at CBS in the late 1960s, Arnold's most ambitious television pilot was a version of his earlier theatrical success The Mouse That Roared. *Sid Caesar reprised the multiple roles played by Peter Sellers in the original, and is here seen as Duchess Gloriana and Prime Minister Montjoy.*

After the success of *The Mouse That Roared,* Arnold had reason to hope that he could attract more feature work — especially comedy. But his agent at the time, Milton Grossman, had reportedly taken one look at *Mouse* and advised Arnold to stick with television, which he more or less did whether he liked it or not. Arnold's prodigious television output through the mid-sixties was punctuated by only two MGM Bob Hope pictures and a teenage race car picture at Universal. When, in 1966, he was offered a lucrative contract as producer-director at CBS, he found the financial temptation too much to resist. "It was probably a mistake career-wise, but CBS needed a trouble-shooter, and they gave me a lot of money for those days. Whenever a program got in trouble they sent me over."

Jack Arnold directing on the set of his Mr. Terrific *television series in the late 1960s. On the left is the show's star, Stephen Strimpell; on the right, actor Dick Gautier.*

Perhaps the best example of this is Arnold's work on the *Gilligan's Island* series. CBS thought the show's creator, Sherwood Schwartz, had a good idea, but the ratings were sagging. Arnold was sent in as producer, working also with the writers and directing episodes. "I knew what it lacked. It wasn't really comedy film; it was like radio writing. I always thought the show should be like the old Mack Sennett two-reelers. I turned it from mere verbal jokes into actions. It was comedy action that came out of the story—in essence, sight gags." Arnold's approach saved the show and brought it up into the top ten in the ratings. "I used to argue with people who would turn up their noses and say, 'Why are you getting involved in such crap?' I said, '*Gilligan's Island* is not crap. It's a show made for young people.' It had some good people in it. The show is not a bad show; it's a good show. It was designed for children. It's fine for its time period and its audience. It wasn't made for intellectuals or to write theses about. It was for kids to enjoy."

While at CBS Arnold also produced and directed a number of pilots including *Who Goes There* and *Mr. Terrific*, the latter of which was made into a series. His most ambitious CBS pilot effort was, however, an adaptation of *The Mouse That Roared*. Arnold had acquired exclusive television rights from author Leonard Wibberley back in 1964 and was now able to interest CBS and Columbia Screen Gems in a co-production deal. This in turn made it possible for him to approach Sid Caesar with a firm offer for a new half-hour color comedy series. Caesar was to play multiple roles as Peter Sellers had done before him in the feature version. The production was a fairly elaborate affair, including the creation of the fictional Grand Duchy of Fenwick, its costumed inhabitants, a U.N. Assembly set, and animated titles by DePatie-Freleng (who did Blake Edwards' *Pink Panther* titles). At a time when American television comedy generally avoided serious satire, Arnold hoped the series might break new ground by tackling controversial subjects in the various episodes. "Our object in all of this," said Arnold in a publicity release, "is to amuse and not to offend, but at least we'll be going into areas which up to the present have been taboo. The trend has been to stay clear of these topics, but the premise of *Mouse* will carry us over a good portion of this sacred ground." The pilot was successfully completed on schedule but never made it to the small screen. It was the standard practice in those days of absolute network hegemony to test pilot shows before an audience at the infamous "Preview House" on Sunset Boulevard. One screening before an unresponsive audience was all it took to kill a show. The *Mouse* pilot was screened, that particular audience was polled, and CBS dropped all plans for the series.

Arnold did not give up, however. In the early fifties he had been a great fan of Sid Caesar's classic *Show of Shows;* he now had the idea of getting the original cast and writers together for a special. "I wanted to see those guys together again. I went to CBS and said, 'Can I see if I can put together a *Show of Shows*?' They said, 'Go ahead if you can do it. You'll never do it.' So I called Sid Caesar and talked to him about doing it. He said, 'I'd love it.' We got most of the original writers except Neil Simon, who was then too big. We paid everybody the same thing — ten thousand dollars."

Opposite, top: *The highlights of Arnold's career as producer-director for CBS was the Emmy-winning* Sid Caesar, Imogene Coca, Howard Morris, Carl Reiner Special, *a reprise of the old* Show of Shows *from the golden age of television. Clutching Emmy Awards, left to right, are Howard Morris, Sid Caesar, Carl Reiner, and Jack Arnold. Bottom: Arnold and his European production associates scouting locations in Italy for the* It Takes a Thief *television series.*

The show aired on April 5, 1967, as *The Sid Caesar, Imogene Coca, Howard Morris, Carl Reiner Special* and was very funny. But behind the scenes things had been otherwise. During production Arnold ran afoul of the network executives over a sketch by Mel Brooks, a take-off on the film *Who's Afraid of Virginia Woolf?* Sid Caesar and Imogene Coca took the roles of Burton and Taylor — Arnold had even gotten Taylor's wig from the film sent over from Warner's.

CBS came to me and said, "You've got to take that out." They said there was too much drinking and the sponsor wouldn't sponsor it. I told them, "That's not drinking; they break bottles — it's slapstick, it's farce." Well, I tell the boys this and they hit the sky. They're not newcomers in show business. So they go to CBS and say, "You don't want to do this? We'll take it to NBC. So f____k you!" CBS said, "Can't you cut down the drinking a little bit?" They said, "We'll see what we can do." At rehearsal — a network lawyer present — we did the same sketch but toned down. We played it for one audience and it didn't play at all. So I said, "Alright, put the sketch back as it originally was." The lawyer glares at me. "And we've got to have Sid or Carl do a warm-up," because we did it without a warm-up. So we invited another audience in and played it the way it was written — Carl and Sid did a warm-up — and everything got laughs. If they burped, it got laughs. But the network wasn't happy. What they were telling me was that Warner's is going to sue us for doing it. And I said, "Warner's is not going to sue us for chrissake. And the sponsor is not going to pull out of the show." I didn't listen to the lawyer. I didn't do what they told me. So when my contract was up, instead of renewing it, they said goodbye. And it was a good thing. But that shows you. It won me the Emmy Award. I said, "What the hell did you want? If I did it the way you wanted it, it would be in the toilet."

As an ironic footnote to this episode, the network called Arnold about a year later, begging him for a copy of the show. The network had apparently lost the master tape in the heat of dissatisfaction and were desperate. Normally Arnold would have kept a copy, but when the network was angry with him he had left everything with them. "It wasn't until we won the Emmy that they realized we were right."

Arnold continued in television, taking over from Frank Price as executive producer and director of *It Takes a Thief* for ABC. Working with the legendary Fred Astaire (whom Arnold recalls as a supreme gentleman and professional), Arnold remodeled the show

Top: *One of the funniest sequences in* Bachelor in Paradise *satirizes suburban supermarkets and shopping housewives. It was shot in the VONS supermarket on Valley Circle Boulevard in Woodland Hills, a fashionable suburb in Los Angeles' San Fernando Valley where Jack Arnold lives today.* Bottom: Bob Hope and Lana Turner in Bachelor in Paradise.

into a considerable success, directing most episodes himself on location in Europe. This extensive foreign location work proved a problem, however, as certain parties took advantage of Arnold's absence to wrest the show from his control.

He continued to direct television through the seventies and into the eighties, taking whatever came his way, including shows like *Love, American Style, Wonder Woman, Fall Guy, Movin' On, Sheriff Lobo,* and *The Love Boat.* In 1979 he directed an NBC "Movie of the Week," *Sex and the Married Woman,* with Barry Newman and Joanna Petit. The following year he co-directed a three hour mini-series, *Marilyn, the Untold Story,* for producer Lawrence Schiller, based on the book by Norman Mailer.

About a year after the highly successful release of the feature *The Mouse That Roared,* Arnold got another feature offer from MGM to direct a comedy feature with two of the biggest stars in the business, Bob Hope and Lana Turner. *Bachelor in Paradise* is a satirical farce about suburban living, with Bob Hope as Adam J. Niles, a writer doing field research in a housing development called "Paradise Estates," in which he becomes the only resident bachelor. This eventually results in his being called as witness in three divorce cases, but he declares his love for Rosemary Howard (Lana Turner), whose home he is renting, and there is a happy ending for all.

In some ways the film is very good. The supporting cast— including Janis Paige, Paula Prentiss, and Agnes Moorehead, among others— is excellent, and the art direction also stands out as a faintly repulsive recreation of suburbia. The problem with *Bachelor in Paradise* is that what began as a smart satire on suburban living was transformed into a romantic vehicle for Bob Hope, with mixed results. As a contemporary reviewer accurately noted,

> When the central plot is kept usefully subservient to these overtones of social commentary, as it is in the early going, the picture roars merrily and infectiously along under Jack Arnold's perceptive surveillance. But as the shallow romantic plot slowly surfaces and the satire sinks, as happens in the latter stages, the complexion of the film changes. Suddenly the undernourished story, which the audience has been tolerating merely as an aid or link to the comic punctuations, takes on an importance beyond its weight.[1]

Those who remember Hope at his best might like the film. After all, he finally, after many years, added Lana Turner to his long and

impressive list of glamorous leading ladies. Viewers of a later generation, however, are more impressed by Jack Arnold's satirical vision
of suburban inanity, and find Bob Hope an unwelcome intrusion.
Produced at the height of suburban expansionism, *Bachelor in Paradise* is still worth watching for this satirical element. Arnold achieved
this in part by letting reality parody itself through adroit use of real
locations. "Paradise Estates" was actually the then-new Woodland
West Homes development in the west San Fernando Valley, and
the hilarious send-up of supermarkets and shopping housewives was
shot nearby in the VONS on Valley Circle Boulevard in Woodland
Hills.

After nearly three years of intervening television work, Arnold
was once again summoned to MGM to direct a Seven Arts–Hal
Bartlett production, *A Global Affair*, again with Bob Hope. The story
is about a minor U.N. functionary left in charge of an abandoned
baby. Since the baby was found in the U.N. it is outside the jurisdic-
tion of the New York welfare services. Hope agrees to turn the baby
over to the "best" country, resulting in some sexy appeals from a bevy
of international beauties. The film ends with Hope giving a sentimental speech to the U.N., proposing the child be the first citizen of the
world.

The film has some good laughs, as when Hope tries to pin the
baby's diaper with scotch tape, and there are some good performances. Michelle Mercier is lovely as the Belgian Hope eventually
marries, and Yvonne De Carlo makes an alluring Spaniard. The real
scene stealers, however, are Swiss-born Lilo Pulver as a Ninotchka-
like Russian and the baby, played alternately by twins Denise and
Danielle Monroe.

However, the film released as *A Global Affair* is not the film that
Jack Arnold made. It was taken from his hands and surreptitiously
altered by the producer, much to its detriment. The problem began
when Bob Hope and MGM insisted on having Jack Arnold as the
director against producer Hal Bartlett's wishes. Arnold recalls his
own version of *A Global Affair* as

*The following two pages show the storyboards for Jack Arnold's opening se-
quence to* A Global Affair. *The sequence as shot was a funny and effective way
to introduce the main character. Inexplicably, however, producer Hal Bartlett
cut it out of the film, leaving the audience in confusion as to who the main
character was.*

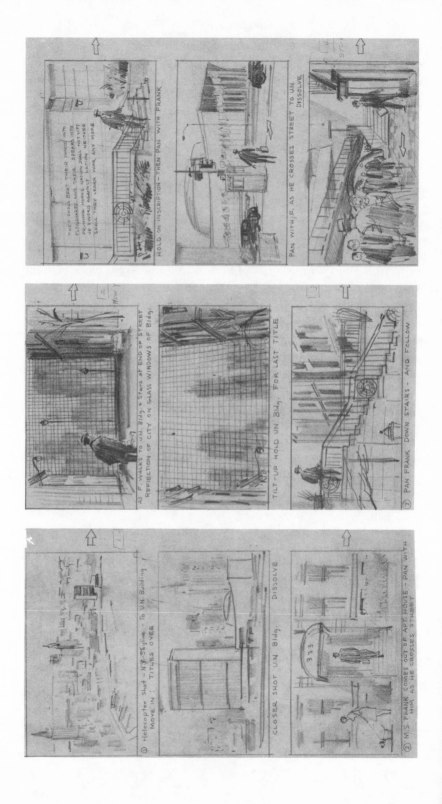

① Helecopter Shot — N.Y. Skyline — To U.N. Building. / MOVE IN. TITLES OVER.

CLOSER SHOT U.N. Bldg.   DISSOLVE

② M.S. FRANK COMES OUT OF APT HOUSE — PAN WITH HIM, AS HE CROSSES STREET

As F. WALKS TO U.N. Bldg., + Stars at END OF STREET / REFLECTION OF CITY ON GLASS WINDOWS OF Bldg.

TILT-UP HOLD U.N. Bldg. FOR LAST TITLE.

③ PAN FRANK DOWN STAIRS — AND FOLLOW

"THEY SHALL BEAT THEIR SWORDS INTO PLOWSHARES AND THEIR SPEARS INTO PRUNING HOOKS, NATION SHALL NOT LIFT UP SWORD AGAINST NATION, NEITHER SHALL THEY LEARN WAR ANY MORE"

HOLD ON INSCRIPTION — THEN PAN WITH FRANK.

PAN WITH F. AS HE CROSSES STREET TO U.N. DISSOLVE

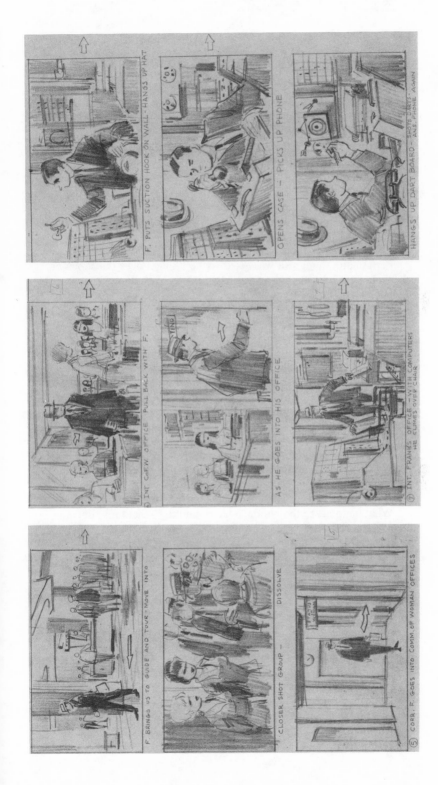

... a tremendously funny film with a lot of content, which was cut so badly after I cut it that I wanted my name taken off. Since then the Directors' Guild has inserted a law that the producer can have his cut, but it has to be approved by the director. After the director finishes cutting the film, and the producer feels inclined to cut it differently, he has to show the director the cut, and they have to agree on it. But they never showed me that cut. I'd finished cutting the film and it was a very good film, believe me, you wouldn't recognize it.

It would have been a great picture if it had been let alone. It's a good picture but not a great picture. It was a well-written script. It's just a crying shame that it had to be ruined.

I showed Bob Hope my cut of *Global Affair* and he was ecstatic, he thought it was great — when he got over the shock of seeing it in black-and-white; he didn't know and the producer hadn't told him. I thought he knew or I would have told him. He hated the producer. Whenever Hal Bartlett came on the stage, he'd go to his dressing room, and he wouldn't come out 'till he left.

This producer ... had the sense of humor of a temporary filling. And he loused up that film. ... Just to give you an indication of how he loused it up: The opening sequence is to establish Bob Hope. Now it's a comedy, if you have Bob Hope you're certainly not making a documentary about anything. The story is a simple story about a child. It was a wonderful premise and a great script. ... It shows you how a wonderful script can be really loused up. A child, an infant is left, abandoned in the United Nations. Now, who has authority over the child? Where does the child go? ... The United Nations doesn't belong to the United States, the cops of New York can't go into the United Nations. What happens to the child? What nation does that child become a ward of? There are one hundred and seventy nations. That was the premise. That is why it was called *Global Affair*. And I designed this opening for the film. I went to New York with Bob to scout locations. I scouted the United Nations and I noticed that if you stand on 44th Street facing the East River, right across the street are the flags of all nations and the towering glass United Nations building. At eleven o'clock the sun reflects the skyline in mosaic in all the windows so that the Empire State Building and all that is recognizable as New York is a mosaic on this building. I said, "That's beautiful. I've got a great opening shot for the film." I started Bob walking down toward the camera on 44th Street, shooting away from the United Nations building. You see a man coming toward you; he's got a homburg hat on, a little flower in his lapel, and his briefcase. He looks like he must be somebody very important — very well dressed. We follow him with a one hundred and eighty degree pan as he turns and goes down the stairs where we see that inscription about "swords into plow-shares." Then I panned up and got that whole line of flags and the reflection of New York and started my titles. Then we see Bob come into the U.N. lobby where they have these pretty young ladies, guides from all countries, who say hello to him in different languages. They're very obsequious to him and say, "Good morning, Sir," that sort of thing. Then we follow him up in an elevator to a huge office with a hundred desks. As he goes past everyone says, "Good morning, Sir," in a different language and you think, "This guy has got to be the head of the United Nations—who the hell is he?" He opens a door and we go right in with him and it's a closet, it's just got a computer in it. And that's his job. He opens his briefcase and takes out his lunch and a dartboard. That was the opening. Then the baby is found. It's late Friday, and everyone has gone leaving Bob as the only official left. So the security police give him the baby and tell him he will have to keep it until Monday morning when the Secretary General and staff return since they can't turn it over to the New York police. He doesn't know what the hell to do with this baby. He lives in an apartment that doesn't allow children. He goes to the pet store and buys a dog carrier to try to sneak the baby past his landlord. The landlord—a pet lover with a big doberman—sees him come in and asks him what kind of animal it is while the doberman ominously sniffs at the carrier. That's how the film begins—it's very funny.

I shot the film, made my cut, and was very happy with the movie. I had screened my cut for Hal Bartlett and he said, "That's fine, just some minor changes. I'll let you know when I'm finished." I said, "Fine, when you're through let me see it." He never called me. Then one day I was down in the publicity department and they say, "Hey, we're running you're film for the press, you want to see it?" I said, "What do you mean you're showing it to the press? I haven't seen what Bartlett's done to it yet." So I hurried into the big screening room and this is how the picture opens: A black screen with a million violins playing; it's break-your-heart-time music. The suddenly up on the screen are faces of starving children of different nations, and that dissolves to the mural in the U.N. lobby where the kid was left and we pan down to the crying baby. With the music and title you think you're watching something about starving kids all over the world! Then the baby is brought to Bob's little office and you don't know who the hell Bob is! I really blew my top. I stormed over to see Maggie, Margaret Booth, head of cutting. I burst into her office mad as hell. I said I wasn't only mad because they didn't show me the picture but also because they ruined it. I told her, "It's not the picture I made—I want my name taken off it. Put anybody's name on or nobody's name, but I want my name off!" I called Bob right away but he was recovering from an eye operation for the eye trouble

Top: *On the U.N. lobby set of* A Global Affair, *Jack Arnold directs a "tour group" that includes his daughter, Susan (far left), who appeared as one of the extras.* Bottom: *Hapless Frank Larrimore (Bob Hope) is caught between the rivalry of international beauties Lisette (Michelle Mercier, left) and Sonya (Lilo Pulver) in this scene from* A Global Affair. *Mercier spoke no English and had to learn her lines one at a time, phonetically.*

In *A Global Affair*, *Bob Hope played harried U.N. computer operator Frank Larrimore; the foundling whose care he undertakes was played in alternate scenes by twins Denise and Danielle Monroe. At top, Frank treats the baby to a drink in his favorite bar. Below, he gives a sentimental speech to the U.N. General Assembly in the final reel.*

he had been developing during shooting. Besides, he wouldn't talk to Bartlett anyway because he hated him.

Bartlett had made trouble right from the start. For instance, Bartlett was supposed to cast the leading lady. Three days into shooting we still had no leading lady—I had to shoot around her. I got a magnum of Champagne for being a day ahead of schedule. Then suddenly we get our leading lady, Michelle Mercier, a beautiful lady who spoke only French, not a word of English. She had to be taught everything phonetically, word by word. I had to cut away every time I came to her so she could learn her next line. I began to fall steadily behind. I complained to Bartlett and asked him why the hell he cast a girl that didn't speak English. "She's beautiful," he said. I said, "She certainly is beautiful, and if our picture was in French it would be wonderful. But our picture's in English and she doesn't speak English!" We had to have a translator there for her to explain the meaning of every line while I just sat there, waiting. Bob nearly went out of his mind. It took a long time, but she did a pretty good job. There was a bright side though. Bob works only with cue cards. We did things so many times he knew his lines by heart so you never see his eyes reading the cards.

But there is more wrong with *A Global Affair* than producer interference, and that is Bob Hope. By the 1960s he was more involved with television than with features, and this lack of commitment showed more as the years went by. "Hope's annual screen endeavors became increasingly erratic, with more bad than good. . . . Such films as *Bachelor in Paradise, Call Me Bwana,* and *A Global Affair* buried Hope's one-time reputation as a reliable movie laugh maker."[2] A veteran Hope staffer recalls, "Even twenty-five years ago I can remember Frank Freeman, who was head of Paramount at the time, trying to tell Bob that he couldn't chase girls anyone, because he was too old, people wouldn't accept it. Twenty-five years later Bob was still chasing girls, and he doesn't realize that he has changed, and you don't get the laughs the way you used to."[3]

Jack Arnold describes his impression of Bob Hope, and a technique he developed while directing him:

> Bob Hope lives in his own world. He comes in, and does his work, and doesn't socialize with any of the cast, which doesn't mean that he's mean, or doesn't joke around with people; it's just that he is a very self-centered gentleman. He doesn't bother to even learn the script, and sometimes, I think, he hasn't read it. . . . It didn't show . . . because I didn't let it show. . . . I had signals with my

From The Lively Set. *At top, James Darren's hair stays perfectly in place as he romances Pamela Tiffin on the grass. At bottom, Pamela Tiffin and Doug McLure appear to be having engine trouble in this on-location race scene.*

cameraman, one of the best in the world [Joseph Ruttenberg]. I
said, "Please, Bob reads from cue cards, on the first two takes we'll
be able to see his eyes reading. . . . I'll want to go over this at least
six times before we do any takes, so will you have your film buckle
or trouble with the lens . . . ? Let's have something go wrong, but
let's go through with it. You don't even have to run any film. I'll
give you a special cue when I want a take." I used that technique
on both pictures I made with Bob Hope.

By the time *A Global Affair* was in release, Jack Arnold had been
called back to Universal by his old friend and associate William
Alland to direct *The Lively Set*. Alland was now on the Universal lot
on a picture-by-picture basis; *The Lively Set* was his penultimate
effort before giving up the film business entirely. Released in the fall
of 1964, *The Lively Set* was Universal's glossy response to AIP's highly
successful "beach party" pictures, but with fast cars replacing surf-
board thrills. James Darren and Pamela Tiffin exert a minor fascination as the wholesome young couple around whom the story revolves, and there are some rock-and-roll numbers, including an appearance by the redoubtable Surfaris. An experimental turbine-
engine car, designed by Chrysler, was also featured as Darren's
brainchild. However, the film's greatest attraction by far is the scenes
of fast cars in action at the Bonneville salt flats and the Tri-State En-
durance Run from Lone Pine, California, to St. George, Utah. Critics
were unanimous in praising Jack Arnold and photographer Carl
Guthrie for creating ". . . race scenes which are as good or better
than anything ever done in the racing line."[4]

In the latter half of 1968 Arnold got an offer from Ivan Tors to
direct an underwater comedy called *Hello Down There*. Arnold had
known Ivan's wife-to-be while still an actor in New York, and met
Ivan through her. Ivan Tors had been very successful, for a number
of years, producing television series like *Sea Hunt, Big Ben,* and *Flip-
per* at his Florida-based studio. He had signed with Paramount to
produce features as well, and *Hello Down There* was the first of these
to be released. The picture attempted something rather difficult in
those days, a G-rated family picture designed to cut across all age
groups and bridge the "generation gap," an idea so old-fashioned as
to seem almost daring.

The premise was, to say the least, unusual. Tony Randall plays
an architect who designs and builds a futuristic underwater house.
His boss, Jim Backus, wants him to destroy it before they become a

Top: *Jack Arnold directing Tony Randall in a scene from* Hello Down There. Bottom: *Richard Dreyfuss makes his film debut leading a rock band called "The Hang-Ups" in* Hello Down There. *Left to right: Gary Tigerman, Lou Wagner, Kay Cole, Dreyfuss.*

laughing stock, but Randall promises to prove its livability by moving in for a month with his aquaphobic wife (Janet Leigh) and their two rock-and-rolling teenage kids. Complications arise when the kids and two of their friends attempt to record a hit record in the underwater house, somehow jamming Navy sonar. Subplots include Ken Berry as Randall's rival with a gold-finding underwater dredge, and Roddy McDowell as a mod record producer named Nate Ashbury who picks his hit records by computer. There are a few underwater thrills with sharks and dolphins, and the film ends with Backus, McDowell and Merv Griffin all showing up in the underwater house to televise the kids' hit song. The whole thing adds up to highly improbable light entertainment.

Arnold enjoyed working for Ivan Tors, for whom he has great respect and affection. As for *Hello Down There,*

> I liked it . . . for what it was. . . . It wasn't going to win any prizes. . . . But I loved the idea of a house underwater, and I loved casting it with the people that we used. We had a lot of fun, Tony Randall and I . . . and the whole cast had a ball down there. . . . We had two dolphins . . . on the set; we had a big set. Ivan had a studio down there in Florida, and he had a big tank, an enormous tank. They got to know I was the boss, so whenever I got near them they used to come up and splash me with water. If I'd come near the edge, they'd come diving up and splash me with their tails.
>
> Paramount didn't think much of it, I don't think, because they gave it a very bad release; they sent it out with some horror picture. This is a picture you could take your grandmother and your three-year-old baby to. We thought as it was a family picture, they should have sold it as a family picture. That's what we made it for. But I know what the trouble was; Ivan had a problem with Paramount. He made a picture prior to this picture; Paramount didn't like it, and wouldn't release it. He had a contract for four more pictures, and they didn't want to honor it, and they were stubborn enough to sabotage the release of *Hello Down There.* It wasn't because they didn't like it, it's because they didn't like Ivan Tors for a reason, which didn't help me any. If they had released the picture right, and given it the publicity it deserved, it would have been a little feather in my cap for doing a little different kind of picture than I usually do. It was a "G" picture and was great for the family. If they'd handled it correctly . . . they could have made money off the picture. They're releasing it now in the ancillary markets and they're doing very well with it.

Much of the atmosphere in Black Eye is due to effective location work. At top, Arnold directs a scene in a seedy area of the beach community in Venice, California. Below, on location in Marina Del Rey, California, Arnold directs a suspenseful sequence in an elevator shaft.

From Black Eye. At top, Arnold with veteran character actor Cyril Delevanti. At bottom, "Jesus Freak" Amy (Jack Arnold's daughter, Susan) explains to private eye Stone (Fred Williamson) that she has found peace and doesn't want to return to her family.

The trouble starts in The Bunny Caper *when Christina Hart (fully dressed, center) makes a bet with her girlfriends to see which of them is the most seductive.*

Arnold's next feature offer came in late 1973 from Pat Rooney, who was producing an adaptation of Jeff Jack's novel *Murder on the Wild Side* for Warner Bros. Entitled *Stone,* the film was to be a Raymond Chandler–style detective story set in Santa Monica and Venice, California.

After the funeral of a silent movie star, a pleasant prostitute (Nancy Fisher) steals a strange silver-headed cane placed on the coffin by the widow, and is afterwards murdered in her Venice apartment. Stone (Fred Williamson) discovers this while visiting his girl friend (Teresa Graves) downstairs, and so is drawn into the intrigue. Meanwhile, a man named Dole (Richard Anderson) hires private eye Stone to find his daugther (Susan Arnold), who is hiding out with a cult of Jesus freaks. The two story lines finally come together with an unusual twist or two in which Stone uncovers a major heroin ring.

Staging and performances are good, but the film's major attraction is its excellent location work; in fact, none of it was shot in a studio. The sleazy ambience of the Venice boardwalk is used to great effect, and there is a spectacular car chase over the Venice canals, reputedly shot surreptitiously without police permits. The director's choice of locations and his ability to work with speed and efficiency contributed considerably to the film's quality. Camera movement is much more fluid than in most films of this type; the zoom lens is little used, and then only in interiors where camera movement was impossible.

Arnold exceeded the producer's expectations in every respect, and brought the picture in two days under schedule. Producer Rooney thanked Arnold publicly in a full-page ad in the *Hollywood Reporter*.

The film is a good detective melodrama, its only real problem being that when released in May, 1974, it had its name changed to *Black Eye*, and was released only as a black exploitation film in the wake of *Shaft*, *Superfly*, etc. Except for the "funkadelic" title theme, and the presence of Fred Williamson, *Black Eye* has little in common with the run of "blaxploitation" pictures. Warner's cashed in on the black film craze of the 1970s, and then promptly forgot about the film. The irony is that *Black Eye* would have probably made more money for Warner Bros. had it not been targeted solely at a black audience.

Shortly after finishing *Black Eye*, Arnold was asked if he would like to direct a modest little comedy film in England. Arnold has had a love affair with England since his days as a stage manager in London's West End and his work on *The Mouse That Roared*. He said yes without even reading the script.

The project, *The Bunny Caper*, turned out to be the latest in a series of similar "girly" films by sleaze producer Peer J. Oppenheimer. British films of this type were tame by American standards, basically a tease with minimal nudity. They were primarily intended for British domestic release.

Oppenheimer had written the script himself, and when Arnold read it he was appalled. It wasn't just the nudity; the comedy itself was poorly written. Arnold asked Oppenheimer if he might do some rewriting and did the best he could to make Oppenheimer's script a little more palatable.

A cast of unknowns was headed by Christina Hart, who made several such films for Oppenheimer. Hart plays a sixteen-year-old nymphomaniac daughter of a United States government official who

Top: *Fred Williamson and D'Urville Martin in* Boss Nigger. Bottom: *William Smith, Fred Williamson, and Jack Arnold during filming of* Boss Nigger.

Senta Berger, David Janssen, and director Jack Arnold on location in the Swiss Alps during filming of The Swiss Conspiracy.

sets international relations on a precarious course when she makes a bet with her girlfriends about which of them could best seduce various diplomats.

Arnold's handling of this material turned exploitation into ribaldry and satire. Stressing the story's comedic qualities, Arnold leaves most of the nudity to the imagination by means of stategically placed foreground objects—a chair back, a lamp shade, a vase of flowers.

He also developed the satirical aspects of the story somewhat. For example, the Russian diplomat is depicted wearing an old-fashioned ankle-length nightshirt to bed, but with all his various medals pinned to his chest.

"I made the film because I love England and enjoy working there. That's the only reason why I took it. I love the English crews, working with them can be a lot of fun. The film is a comedy and it turned out to be very funny. But it's not a good picture. There is some nudity in it, so I'm not bragging about it." But it was not a total loss. In effect, Arnold made *The Bunny Caper* a working vacation, all

expenses paid. He even took the opportunity to visit his favorite London tailor and had a new gray herringbone lounge suit made.

The reviews were generally favorable. The nudity was negligible
by Unites States standards, and the film was simply regarded as an
R-rated youth comedy in the States. One reviewer noted, "Long time
Hollywood director Jack Arnold has guided his talented cast in a
high-comedy manner."[5] *The Bunny Caper* did well in its British
domestic release, and had a brief American release in the summer of
1974.

In mid–1974 Arnold co-produced and directed an independent
production starring Fred Williamson and D'Urville Martin entitled
Boss Nigger, a western directed in economical B-movie style. The
original screenplay, written by Williamson with additions and am-
mendations by Arnold, is a satire on the traditional B-western formula of the bounty hunter taking over the job of sheriff and cleaning
up the town.

Arnold seems to have been more the *artiste exécutant* on this picture; content-wise, we must regard Fred Williamson as the film's
auteur. He is like a black Clint Eastwood in a Catafavi western.
Williamson's bounty hunter turns the tables on the town's white
establishment with an intelligent and biting wit. He is very popular
in the nearby Mexican village and is generous to its inhabitants—a
kind of cinematic third-world unity. From an ideological standpoint,
it is interesting to note that the only white male who turns out to be
worth much is the blacksmith, a simple, honest tradesman. The
banker and mayor, however, are villainous. William Smith (a born B-
movie actor if there ever was one, known for biker films and star of
Invasion of the Bee Girls the year before) excels as the desperado in
cahoots with the mayor.

In some ways *Boss Nigger* is an amazing film. It was shot in the
western town on the Eves Ranch in New Mexico on a budget of
$200,000. The full-scope Todd-AO 35 photography is good, and the
camera movement and staging are excellent. No corners appear to
be cut. Yet Jack Arnold's major contribution to this film is that it was
made at all; only a director with his experience and efficient technique could have made so much out of so little. He did not hesitate
to do whatever was necessary to get the film made, including doing
wound make-up on his actors and actually helping dig a needed
"grave" in the desert heat!

Boss Nigger was released in January, 1975, and did very well, getting uniformly good reviews. Vincent Canby of the *New York Times* wrote, *"Boss Nigger* . . . is the kind of unpretentious ramshackle movie that can be a pleasant surprise if you stumble upon it without warning."[6]

The following year Arnold began work on an American–West German co-production, *The Swiss Conspiracy,* a tale of intrigue involving secret numbered bank accounts. Maurice Silverstein, former head of MGM in Europe, sent him the script, which needed a lot of work. Arnold took care of the rewrite himself and assembled an impressive cast including David Janssen, Senta Berger, John Ireland, Ray Milland, Elke Sommer, and John Saxon. Shooting began in May, 1975.

The finished film has good performances and a very good look—the color photography is beautiful. One reviewer noted, "A cast of familiar names and some gorgeous locale filming contribute to make this . . . an exciting cliffhanger. There is sufficient intrigue, murder and blackmail to keep the audience guessing. Jack Arnold is at home with suspense . . . . The screenplay . . . revolves around secret bank accounts in Zurich and six people being blackmailed to protect their secrets. Everyone appears to be on the shady side and no one is above suspicion. The dialog is to the point and action scenes are exciting, whether it is a car chase or a ride on a ski lift. The scenery is breathtaking."[7]

Unfortunately, something happened on the way to being released. The American investors had made the film especially as a tax shelter and apparently sabotaged the United States release. Originally announced as a Warner's release, it was acquired by Salah Jammal's S.J. International Pictures and released in May, 1977; then it quietly vanished.

This caused something of a scandal at the time. A banner headline in *Variety* reads "9 TAX SHELTER PIX FACE LEGAL AUTOPSY, Misuse of Funds Judgement Awaited." Producer Silverstein and his partner Raymond R. Homer were sued for $45,000,000 in a federal court. As *Variety* noted, "None of the films, some of which remain uncompleted, have ever played New York City and only one . . . was ever tradescreened."[8]

However, the German co-producer Lutz Hengst, head of Bavaria studios, liked the film and had always intended to make money with it. He got a good release through Columbia-Warner (Europe) in May 1976, and the film did very well in Europe. This did not improve things much for Arnold back in the States. His film disappeared and went virtually unnoticed. "It's too bad," said Arnold, "because you work very hard on something, you get to be proud of it, then old man greed comes along . . ."

The Swiss Conspiracy was to be Jack Arnold's last theatrical feature.

8
A Lost World

In the annals of art there are many attempted masterworks that never saw completion. Michelangelo's designs for the vast tomb of Pope Julius II and Dickens' *The Mystery of Edwin Drood* are random examples that come to mind. The motion picture medium is no different in this regard. One has only to remember Eisenstein's frustrated Mexican project on which he labored so long, Ruben Mamoulian's sound version of *R.U.R.*, Fritz Lang's *Tomorrow*, Willis O'Brien's *War Eagles* and *Creation;* the list is seemingly endless. While it is perhaps true that many shelved films were not worth making, one cannot but be intrigued by the remains of certain unrealized projects by artists of special vision and talent. Moreover, in the area of film specifically, where cost often imposes severe commercial constraints, it may be the unfinished project—perhaps too personal to find adequate support—that reveals the most about an artist. From this perspective we may wish to consider some of the projects on which Jack Arnold long struggled but was regrettably unable to bring to completion. The most significant of these is without doubt the project on which he was working before his present retirement, a science-fiction story and an elegant period piece, the definitive retelling of Sir Arthur Conan Doyle's *The Lost World*.

Arnold had read *The Lost World* years before and realized that as a fantastic tale of high adventure and suspense it had strong cinematic potential. Four English explorers journey up an uncharted Amazonian tributary toward an unknown and mysterious goal. They are surrounded by the incessant drumming of unseen primitive tribes. Will they find the lost plateau? Will they escape the treachery of their vengeful servant Gomez? How will they survive the unknown

166

terrors of this prehistoric world? What hideous fate awaits them at the hands of the loathsome ape-men? Is there no means of escape from the plateau? Will they be able to convince the world of the truth of their discoveries? Conan Doyle brings these suspenseful proceedings to a swift and satisfying conclusion with a number of suspenseful plot twists. How will Gladys welcome Ned, who had embarked on the adventure to win her favor? What will happen when Prof. Challenger confronts the skeptics with his discoveries at the great meeting in Queen's Hall? At last we learn what was in the mysterious packing case he brought back from the plateau as Challenger displays a living pterodactyl which promptly escapes in the confusion!

Yet Conan Doyle's story is more than mere suspenseful adventure with a science fiction premise. It must be remembered that this now over-familiar premise of explorers lost in a prehistoric setting *originated* in *The Lost World* and that Conan Doyle was writing within living memory of the great evolution-versus-creation controversy of the latter half of the nineteenth century. The word "dinosaur" itself was scarcely more than a half-century old, and the whole concept of those great prehistoric monsters was just beginning to take its present place in the landscape of the popular imagination. The great paleontological collections of Chicago, New York, and London were a recent phenomenon, and their display to the public in natural history museums was still causing a sensation. In fact, it was just at this time that the first truly accurate reconstructions of dinosaurs were being made, primarily by the painter and sculptor Charles R. Knight, whose pioneering work is still to be seen in most major museums, and whose vision of prehistoric life dominates our conception of dinosauria to this very day. Indeed, Conan Doyle's conception of these creatures was in some respects not quite state-of-the-art in his own day. Knight's reconstructions were just a little too new: Conan Doyle's Allosauri, for example, portrayed as they are like huge, malevolent, tailed, carnivorous, bipedal toads, seem to owe more to the Victorian reconstructions of sculptor Waterhouse Hawkins. Despite these slight flaws, however, Conan Doyle's imaginary confrontation with these monsters is nonetheless very dramatic and highly effective.

The Lost World also goes beyond adventure and the startling recreation of prehistoric life by making a few sly points about society and civilization. Though the characterization of the explorers' black manservant "Zambo" may seem in some ways patronizing by today's

standards, Conan Doyle expresses his objection to the Spanish en-
slavement of Indians and portrays Lord Roxton as using his inherited
wealth and position to combat it. The dignity of the aboriginal
peoples is upheld throughout, the conceit of Professor Challenger
going so far at one point as to say that a particular tribe is so primitive
that they are "scarcely more intelligent than the average Londoner."
Indeed, the civilized nature of these so-called "primitive" tribes is ex-
pressly brought out in the final confrontation with the ape-men, in
which our explorers naturally take sides with the Indians. The dogmatic stubbornness of some supposed men of science is also brought
in for attack. There seems to be a quiet snub of the Christian funda-
mentalist view of prehistory as well, inasmuch as the entire story
assumes the validity of paleontological science and the theory of
evolution. One might add that, given the present recrudescence of
fundamentalism, the truth of the paleontological view of prehistory
is once again a timely issue.

It is thus easy to see why *The Lost World* was so attractive to a
storyteller of Jack Arnold's sensibilities, but he was by no means the
first to see its cinematic potential. Within a decade of the book's appearance American film producer Watterson Rothacker had acquired the rights with the intention of producing a feature. The dinosaurs were to be created by the young Willis O'Brien using the then-
experimental stop-motion technique. Rothacker arranged to co-
produce the feature with First National Pictures at their Burbank lot.
The flexible dinosaur animation models were constructed by gifted
Mexican sculptor Marcel Delgado. Delgado's designs were definitely
an advance over Conan Doyle's book as they were based on the reconstructions of Charles R. Knight. Inspired casting featured
Wallace Beery as Professor Challenger. The screenplay kept fairly
close to the book with a few notable exceptions. The tribe of ape-men
becomes one sufficiently menancing ape-man, doubtless for reasons
of economy. The escape from the plateau is portrayed as a positively
apocalyptic sequence, with dozens of dinosaurs fleeing an erupting
volcano—a concept later copied in numerous films of this genre. The
film also has Challenger bring back a brontosaurus rather than a
mere pterodactyl, a choice more than justified by the monster's
dramatic rampage through the streets of London. The prints were
also beautifully tinted: greenish for jungles, reddish for the volcanic
eruption, ochre for the gas-lit interior of the science academy, blue
for the London streets at night, etc. Released originally as ten reels in

1925, *The Lost World* was given the deluxe roadshow treatment and was a considerable success. Even today the screening of a well-preserved archival print—projected at the correct speed with the proper musical accompaniment—never fails to delight and thrill a receptive audience. Its very age, however, and the fact that it is silent, makes it something of an artifact in today's world. The desirability of a modern sound and color version is obvious.

It is a regrettable fact that an awful modern sound and color version of *The Lost World* has already been made. Indeed, many people have never heard of the silent version (much less Conan Doyle's book), and the many negative qualities of this later film have done much to obscure the importance of this classic story. Released in 1960, Irwin Allen's version of *The Lost World* is an abominable travesty in every respect. First of all, the film is an update; no attempt was made to create the necessary period atmosphere. (In this regard Arnold has stated that the story might be given ". . . a modern touch without being out of period. It's set in 1912 or 1910, a period piece. You can't update it or it won't play. It's atmosphere that you're playing when you're doing this kind of thing. You must create the atmosphere.") The great Claude Rains (in one of his last roles) is wasted as Challenger, while Michael Rennie, Fernando Lamas, and David Hedison embarrass themselves throughout with inane dialogue and predictable plot developments. Jill St. John is sent along to be menaced by a giant spider and man-eating plants. Producer Allen later recycled footage of Hedison battling the giant spider in his equally juvenile *Voyage to the Bottom of the Sea* television series. The "prehistoric" creatures are a tarantula and pet shop iguanas (with phony rubber fins) clumsily matted into the scenes by means of blue-screen technique, jiggling blue matte outlines abounding. If this was not sufficient insult to all concerned, Allen actually put the venerable Willis O'Brien in the credits as "technical consultant." On the positive side, however, one might regard this film's mere existence as a powerful incentive to create a new and definitive version of Conan Doyle's original story.

It was in early 1982, while Arnold was still working on pre-production for the intended 3-D remake of *Creature from the Black Lagoon* at Universal, that plans for this new version of *The Lost World* began to take shape. In Arnold's words:

I had long wanted to do another science-fiction picture and longed to create something of enduring value rather than just copying myself with a remake of *Creature* like the studio wanted. To this end I re-read Sir Arthur Conan Doyle's *The Lost World*. Then one day in the commissary at Universal I saw Albert Whitlock. He came over to my table, introduced himself, and said he had heard about me and wanted to meet me. Of course I had heard about him; he's probably the best special effects matte man in the world. It wasn't long after that we enthusiastically agreed that it would be a hell of an idea for the two of us to remake Doyle's *The Lost World*.

The idea was that Whitlock and Arnold would co-produce, with Arnold directing. This was to be Whitlock's first experience as a producer, but there was no doubt that he was to play an essential creative role. In fact, he had long nurtured a desire to remake *The Lost World* as the perfect showcase for his considerable genius as a matte artist. His great talent in this field is legendary, and his list of film credits both numerous and impressive. During his long tenure at Universal his paintings have added scope and atmosphere to a great many pictures, including most of those done there by Hitchcock, as well as more recent effects blockbusters like *Earthquake* and *The Towering Inferno*. While Whitlock had been well compensated financially for his efforts, he was nonetheless merely making art to order. None of these projects allowed him to express the true magnitude of his talent, not only in its technical perfection but also in his ability to create atmosphere. This is what a project like *The Lost World* would provide.

It is perhaps appropriate briefly to mention here what is probably the best work done along these lines before Whitlock began creating paintings for a new version of *The Lost World*. In the early 1930s Merian C. Cooper and Ernest B. Schoedsack co-produced and directed *King Kong*, a development of the theme of a lost prehistoric world, utilizing the talents of Willis O'Brien and Marcel Delgado (who had done the effects on the silent *The Lost World* just a few years previously). It is without doubt O'Brien's greatest work and is considered by many to be a true masterpiece of twentieth century art. To create the sustained primeval atmosphere required for much of the film, a great number of matte-paintings and glass-shots were used, many of them created by artists Byron Crabbe and Mario Larrinaga. Inspired by the lighting effects in the engravings of nineteenth century illustrator Gustave Doré, the work of these artists was essential to the successful creation of atmosphere in *King*

Kong. By contrast, the utter absence of this technique (and such artistic sensitivity) is one of many flaws of the absurd 1976 Dino DeLaurentiis remake. It is undoubtedly the kind of effect achieved by Crabbe and Larrinaga in the original *King Kong* that Albert Whitlock wished to emulate and surpass.

It was now up to Arnold to get the project moving. He had been working for some time with screenwriter Gene Ayres on presentations for various projects, and it was natural for him to turn to Ayres for collaboration on this one. Ayres recalls his first involvement:

Jack invited me over to lunch one day (at Universal) to meet Al Whitlock. Al had apparently been wanting to do this book for a long time, and Jack introduced me as a screenwriter he wanted to work with. We talked, and Al said "Great! What we have to do is pitch it to the studio." Al gave me a copy of the book which I read and studied. He wanted to do a period piece true to the feeling of Doyle, but said to let my imagination go. Jack agreed. So I came up with a four page presentation in the form of a letter from the main character Ned Malone stranded on the plateau; he had sent it back by Indians and was unsure if it would ever reach its destination. Well, they went for it. Jack and Al presented this to Ned Tannen along with some of Al's first paintings and Ned said "go." I had injected a few elements. I had come from being into comedy and also into action-adventure, particularly animation where there are fewer limits than in live-action. Al was encouraging me not to worry about budget because he and Jack would figure a way to do it with ingenious effects. I had been to this region of South America, not far from where the Incas made their last stand. I thought it would be interesting if the American Maple White had been looking for the lost city of the Incas, which was discovered by American Hiram Bingham in 1912 — the year in which this story takes place. Bingham was there about the time the book was published; Doyle had apparently missed out by a year or so — so why not give it to him? I'm sure he would have used it. Maple White had been looking for the lost city of the Incas and had found the plateau instead. So there was this whole thing about the Inca treasure. I made the plateau Indians Incas instead. The Incas were up there because there was nowhere else for them to go after they escaped from Pizarro.

On following pages, excerpts from the storyboards derived from the earliest version of Gene Ayres' script for The Lost World. *In this version, the explorers wander through an Inca labyrinth and find the lost treasure of the Incas.*

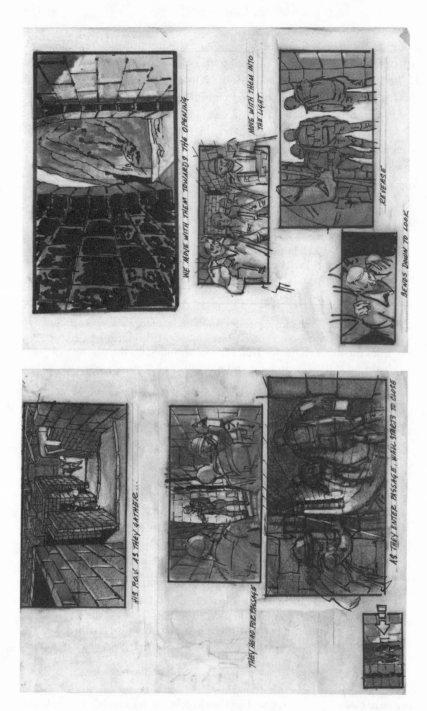

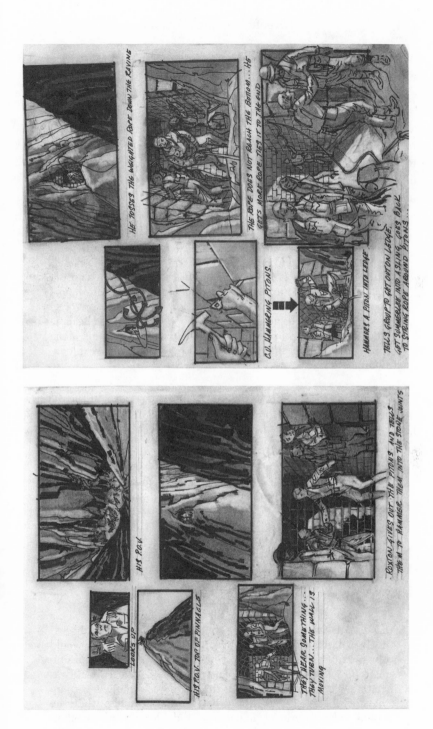

Although there were pre-production drawings and storyboards made using the Inca idea, it was ultimately set aside in favor of a concept closer to the book.

Another concern was whether or not there should be a woman along on the expedition. A commercial film of this type is virtually required to have some love interest, and monsters without a woman to menace are to some minds almost unthinkable. Yet the addition of a woman posed problems of credibility and taste. Such an addition might easily devolve into cliché. As Ayres recalls:

> When we first started boarding this we screened the old Michael Rennie version. It was the old '50s cliche, really pointless. If you're doing a period piece would you really contrive to have a woman along? And it is not in the original story. There is a hostile relationship—a battle of the sexes—going on between Malone and his fiancée back in England which is his motivation for going. If a woman was to be added one would hope that it would be done somewhat like Sigourney Weaver in *Aliens* or something along those lines so it doesn't look like another Raquel Welch exploitation-type image.

Arnold worked in close collaboration with Ayres in the script's development. While giving the writer a free hand in some respects, he did not hesitate to assert himself when necessary to get what he wanted. According to Ayres:

> Jack was most interested in specific scenes. Being a director he saw how a scene should be and seemed more concerned about this than about the overall structure of the story. I remember one thing about which Jack got very emphatic. He wanted to build more suspense during the trip up the Amazon. He wanted a scene in which it looks like the explorers are being attacked by headhunters, but it turns out that the "headhunters" are just peddlers selling fake heads. Jack wanted this as a build up to the scene where they are really attacked by headhunters.
>
> We worked together very closely, and discussed things on a day-to-day basis. I would write something and we would discuss it. He would make his comments or suggestions on how he would like to structure something to shoot it. Also, being the consummate director's director, the true director that he is, Jack was waiting to get his teeth into this thing. He was waiting to get into the storyboards and take the project to the next step where he would make his primary impact. We did a lot of work together, and worked together well. It wasn't that I wouldn't argue with

him, but he was usually right, a man of great experience. I could be right in a sense about a certain scene or story structure because I am a writer and I understand writing. But he would usually be right when it came down to "Can we shoot this? How is it going to play on the screen?" I learned a lot from him in that process.

Arnold is a director who likes to work with writers in strong collaboration, insuring that the cinematic qualities are in the script from its inception. Arnold instinctively prefers to structure a film around a series of strong vignettes that carry the story forward visually, one unfolding after the other. The plot and dialogue are something for the writer to weave around and through those basic visual strengths. As screenwriter Ayres explains:

> That's the way he worked with me. He would have a tableau or scene he wanted that would strengthen the story. In stepping back I could see that, for example, the surprise of the fake head-hunters does strengthen the suspense. When the real attack happens it catches you unaware because you've already been through one where it didn't really happen. Jack would look for certain things he would want there and the rest he would leave to me. That is, until we got to the final editing; then he'd go over everything word by word. He would have a few things he wanted, I would go and write it, then he would sit down with me and say, "Alright now, let's talk about this scene." Scene by scene, line by line, we'd go over the whole thing.

As the script took shape, Arnold began sketching storyboards for the many critical action and effects sequences. Co-producer Whitlock was also far from idle, producing quite a few pre-production paintings of eerie beauty. In due time the script was completed and at last submitted to the studio heads—who promptly asked for a rewrite. This is, of course, the normal and expected practice at Universal, and is one of the many ways in which the studio imposes its will on the artists it employs. *The High Road to China*, a vehicle for actor Tom Selleck, was in production at the time, and the studio assigned its writer, Sandra Weintraub, to do the rewrite on *The Lost World*.

Weintraub's script, co-authored with her husband Anthony C. Roland, is a complete departure from both the book and the original script. The story now revolves around a new central character, Samantha Maple-White, to have been played perhaps by Jane

Seymour. Samantha is supposed to be Professor Challenger's niece and the daughter of the ill-fated Maple-White, discoverer of the lost plateau. (American artist Mr. Maple White of Conan Doyle's original story has his first and last names hyphenated to become an English explorer with the surname Maple-White.) Samantha finances the expedition to vindicate her father's name and serves as love interest for our bumbling hero Ned Malone—there's a few sexy scenes. Samantha also strikes up a relationship with a cute little dinosaur (a "cosmognathus"), whom she calls "little Cosmo." When Sam is not feeding it cookies it squeaks and follows her around like a puppy, its head wistfully cocked to one side. There is also a "cat fight" between Samantha and a young Indian vixen over Ned's affections. In the end our explorers escape by means of a hot air balloon made from an inflated dinosaur stomach during an apocalyptic final confrontation between the Indians and the ape-men with a marauding Allosaurus thrown in to add to the mayhem. A fantastic adventure in the Hollywood mold, Weintraub and Roland's script may be *a* lost world, but it is certainly not *The Lost World* of Sir Arthur Conan Doyle.

Arnold thought for a time that he might make this version work, though he did express some reservations. After due consideration and long discussions with co-producer Whitlock, it was decided that there should be another rewrite, this time more faithful to the original story. It was assigned to the writing team of Ellen Brown and Anita Russel, although the revised first draft also credited Gene Ayres for "additional dialogue." This script is, on the whole, a meticulously literal adaptation of Conan Doyle's book, following the plot and characterizations closely. In fact, the dialogue is in some places almost taken word for word from Conan Doyle. There are, however, a few innovations. Our hero Ned Malone has become "Edward," and Challenger now has a daughter of marriageable age, Lucy. Although a woman's presence on such an expedition is a bit farfetched for a story set in this period, the character of Lucy is intruded with reasonable restraint and credibility. Nonetheless, her appearance in the story is primarily to provide the love interest for our hero Malone.

All now seemed well, but the project was in for a major setback. Ned Tannen left Universal and was succeeded as production head by Bob Rehme, late of Corman's New World Pictures. Rehme saw *The Lost World* as utterly out of place in Universal's production lineup and killed all plans for the project. Rehme's tenure at Universal was,

however, mercifully brief. When Frank Price came in from Columbia to replace him the project was restored—this time with John
Landis as executive producer.

Director Landis had made a number of successful films for Universal, and his involvement as executive producer of *The Lost World*
seemed to considerably strengthen its chances for success. He also
had experience shooting in England only a few years before *(An
American Werewolf in London)* which might have proved helpful as
both the beginning and end of *The Lost World* take place in London.
Landis sent the script to an English writer of his acquaintance, John
Fortune, for a final polishing and set his English production manager
to work preparing the budget.

Arnold, meanwhile, was storyboarding the entire script, and
even added a number of suspenseful action sequences not found in
the script. (These final storyboards, beautifully rendered by clean-up
artist Mentor Heubner, reveal Arnold's penchant for careful planning
and display his superb directorial sense at its very best. The story is
unfolded *visually* and is truly cinematic inasmuch as there is little
dependence on dialogue.) Arnold also began listing and working out
the technical details of all scenes requiring dinosaur effects, and
made contact with stop-motion animators Jim Danforth and Dave
Allen. However, the major challenge now confronting Arnold was
not the technical effects work but the budget. The studio was in-
sisting on an above-the-line budget of only $10 million—absurdly
lean for a period piece of such epic scope. But Arnold had a strate-
gem, which he explained at the time in this way:

> We're doing all the master shots, the long shots with the mattes
> first, with doubles, so that we will use the actors relatively fewer
> days than normal, so that our shooting schedule won't be as long
> as a normal picture of this type. No picture has been made this
> way. We're pioneering it. I don't think it could be done without
> a talent like Al Whitlock. He's a fine man and a great artist. . . .
> He's made some paintings already; they are just beautiful. As soon
> as we're satisfied with the script we'll start casting. I expect to
> spend a couple of weeks in England; I want to get English
> actors. . . . Since all the long shots will already be done, all I'll
> need them for is the close-ups and the medium shots. So it's an
> experiment in a sense, since it's never been done on this scale
> before.

Co-producer Whitlock had by now done a great deal of location
scouting and had settled on some wild terrain in the state parks of

North Carolina. These natural settings in which the actors would move were to be greatly enhanced and expanded by Whitlock's artistry to create the film's lost Amazonian plateau. Whitlock prepared detailed maps and took numerous photographs. The French Broad River was to double for the Amazon, with Chimney Rock and Pilot Mountain standing in for sections of the lost plateau. The desirability of these locations was further enhanced by the proximity of the Earl Owensby Studio, a complete modern facility that could provide both location services and studio "green sets" for close-up dialogue.

John Fortune's final rewrite arrived from England in May of 1984 to the general satisfaction of all concerned. Arnold at last had a script he could work with. The only obstacle now was the budget. Unlike Jack Arnold, John Landis is not used to ingenious filmmaking on tight budgets, and when the budget arrived it was too high—$10 million below-the-line, that is, excluding the acting talent. Jack Arnold recalls:

> What killed our effort was that John Landis brought in an English production manager used to doing An American Werewolf in London or whatever where money was not such a problem. He came up with a below-the-budget of ten million—and it was supposed to be cheaper to do in London than here! The studio said they'd only go ten million above-the-line tops. I wanted to fight and say "Look, let me go over this thing with him because I'm sure he's out of his head and I'll show him where he can cut corners."

But as luck would have it, Arnold found himself hospitalized for a while just when the budget was being submitted to the studio brass. John Landis was abroad at the time and may have had distractions of his own with the aftermath of a dreadful accident on the set of The Twilight Zone, where several people were killed when a helicopter crashed on the set during filming. The result was that the studio quietly dropped all plans for The Lost World. Commerce had once again triumphed over art.

Jack Arnold once said with regard to The Lost World that he only wanted "half a chance." Now even that half-chance would be denied him—to the loss of everyone. His friend and collaborator Gene Ayres expressed this in the following way:

> Jack had made his whole career in doing the little pictures—little pictures with a small budget and a big impact. I don't think he

really had a chance to do an A picture. This would have been one. Even though there were tremendous budget constraints, because of the combined skills involved, this was going to be an A picture. He saw, we all saw — and he would have been the man who would really put it together — that it would have been his chance to create an enduring classic. It would have been one of *the* classic adventure pictures; the definitive version, *this* story the way it should have been done in the first place, the way it can be done, the way it could have been done. It would have been an A picture; it would have been done with taste and style and all that stuff that he can do that no one had really let him do except in very rare circumstances and almost accidentally like *The Mouse That Roared*. . . . *The Lost World* would have had all the elements and I think that's how he saw it and wanted to do it. It would have been the crowning achievement of his career. . . . It is the big picture he almost made.

The great irony is that the studio chiefs of the time didn't know what a great thing they had here. I don't think they even noticed that this project came and went. That's a tremendous irony, really. We all believed we had a real classic picture in the making. But they were busy with films like *The Blues Brothers* and *The High Road to China*. Of the pictures they were making that year not one has survived, but that's where they were, that's what they were doing. It's their business. The summer that we were developing this picture, summer of '82, the only movie that was being shot on the Universal lot at the time was *Doctor Detroit*, and they were getting ready to do *The High Road to China*.

The Lost World is one of those projects that could and should have been done — that would have been great.

There is no one working in Hollywood today that could do this picture except Jack Arnold. Nobody else has that right combination of sensitivity to story and character, ability to do something on a shoestring, *and* the ability to give it the big look. Those three combined qualities, I don't see anyone out there who has them, and I don't think you'll see anyone for a long time. What you're getting now are people out of MTV, commercials, and film school — they're mere technical experts. If this picture gets re-made by someone else in the future it will be a big-budget special effects thing with shallow characters and relationships. I could be wrong, but I think if there is a re-make it will be just like the Michael Rennie version but with a bigger effects budget.

There is a considerable fascination in that which never was. As we now sift through the remaining notes, memoranda, scripts, storyboard sketches, etc., we can try to imagine the pleasure of watching Jack Arnold's *The Lost World*, a film that almost was. With characteristic modesty Arnold said, "It would have been a good picture."

Reproduced on the following pages is a selection of Jack Arnold's final storyboards for The Lost World, *as rendered by clean-up artist Mentor Heubner.*

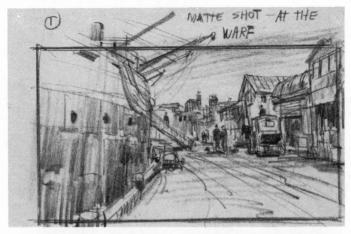

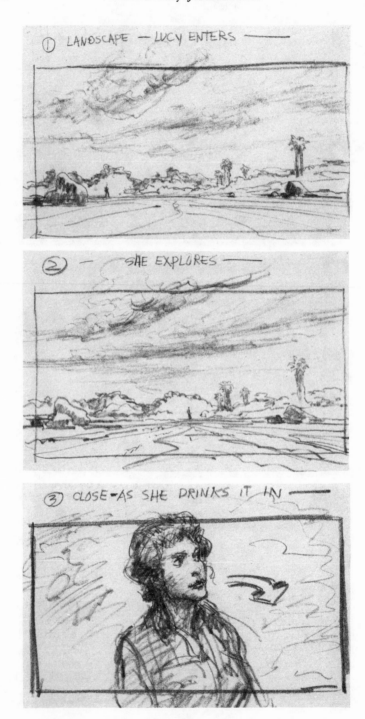

7) CHALLENGER YELLS FOR HIS DAUGHTER ——

8) LUCY HEARS THE CALL ——

9) MONSTER WATCHES HER GO ——

① MAIN AUDITORIUM — ALBERT HALL —

② CHALLENGER TAKES THE PODIUM —

⑤ ROAR OF RESPONSE FROM THE CROWD —

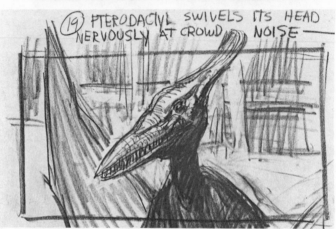

9
The Art of the Storyteller

In the more than thirty years covered, we have seen some of the difficulties and opportunities Jack Arnold encountered working within the Hollywood system. We find that the degree to which he was able to express his artistic personality varied considerably from almost total directorial control, as with *The Incredible Shrinking Man*, to an uncomfortable degree of producer domination, as with *A Global Affair*. Often it was the smallest films that offered him the least producer and studio pressure. Confronted with small budgets, tight schedules, but relative freedom, Arnold responded by developing an extremely organized and efficient directorial manner, maximizing his resources and making the most of the degree of freedom he had. *Outside the Law* and *The Space Children* are marked examples of this. By way of contrast, the star vehicles on which he worked cramped his style, and made personal creativity more difficult. For example, in *The Lady Takes a Flyer*, Arnold was sympathetic to the needs of Lana Turner with regard to special lighting and camera angles, but found it a time-consuming annoyance occasionally at odds with what he might have wanted for particular shots. Arnold's work with Bob Hope is an even more extreme example: The many takes required to rehearse Hope on his cue cards made spontaneity difficult.

Another variable that affected the potential for self-expression in Jack Arnold's work was the quality of the stories that came his way. From our overview we can see that some stories provided him with greater latitude for personal expression than others, and that he sought full expression by pushing subjects that intrigued him (and whose ideas were congruent with his own) to their very limits. Thus

193

The Mouse That Roared became for him a personal statement on social and political issues, while *The Incredible Shrinking Man* reveals his intuitive knowledge of the eternal origin of the human soul. Finding stories with meaningful content was not always easy, especially when one was working in the often heartless context of commercial filmmaking. Sometimes one was fortunate enough to attract good material to oneself; often one had to accept whatever came along as part of the practical necessity of making one's livelihood. This has been very much the case with Jack Arnold, especially in the last two decades, during which he has been primarily occupied by the undistinguished task of television direction, and few feature projects worthy of his talents have come to him.

Perhaps Edward Muhl and the other production executives at U-I should be given credit for assigning Arnold to as many good projects as they did; it can hardly be an accident that he was assigned to so many science-fiction films, which are among his best. That these films benefitted from his direction is evinced by comparing the Arnold-Alland science-fiction films such as *Creature from the Black Lagoon* and *Tarantula!* with the Alland productions directed by others, like *The Mole People* and *The Deadly Mantis*. Budgets and production values are comparable, and the superiority of the former due to the director.

It was in the crucible of B-movie production at Universal-International that Arnold developed his characteristic directorial style and technique. Among the more remarkable skills he developed are his speed and low shooting ratios; Arnold plans everything carefully and is able to get what he wants with a minimum of wastage. This has made him popular as a director who is pulled in at the last minute to save a botched job. (Notable examples are his uncredited redirection of sequences in *The Land Unknown* and *This Island Earth*.) His reputation for lean efficiency actually prompted one producer to offer him five percent of every dollar under budget in lieu of a ten-thousand dollar advance. Confident that Arnold could bring the picture in under budget and ahead of schedule, the producer wrote, "I personally believe that the bonus offer could be highly desirable from your point of view and I am sure that with the corners you can cut through your experience you will not hurt the picture but would be able to make yourself a fairly considerable amount of extra money." Yet this very efficiency and acute mastery of the practical aspects of filmmaking may have kept him from attracting certain

Jack Arnold speaking before a large crowd of appreciative fans at the 1982 Sci-Fi X-po in Seattle, Washington.

projects of quality. "It may have hurt me. . . . It may have given me a reputation of being so fast that I couldn't do justice to the material. I think they're wrong. . . . I regret that it's possible." But it runs against Arnold's grain to waste resources as costly as those needed to make a motion picture.

> Unfortunately, I was brought up that way. I was brought up to be responsible. And when a studio made me responsible for a million dollars, I couldn't in all conscience go over that amount. And I work very diligently in preparation so I don't have to ad lib anything when I get on the stage. I know what I'm going to do for the next forty days if it's a forty-day schedule because I've already had it drawn up. I sit with my art director and I do a storyboard on every scene. . . . When you know what you want, you save a lot of time. There are a lot of directors in this town who read the script a couple of times and that's their preparation. They come on the set and look around, and say, well, let's go over here and we'll do a master from over here and then they'll spend an awful lot of time. Meanwhile, I could have done about three days' work by the time they get one day's work done.
>
> Some of these big films that they spend so much money on I think are such a waste.

I remember setting up a master shot [in *Outside the Law*] that I'd worked out, I'd worked about a week working out this master shot; the scene was important. It was between the cop [Onslow Stevens] and Ray [Danton]. I had thirty-seven moves with the dolly that had to be done.... Once I did that I'd gotten rid of about eight pages of script. One shot . . . it was very good, very effective, you didn't miss anything.

Much of Arnold's accomplishment is not evident on the screen because most viewers have no idea how quickly and economically he shot many of his films.

Arnold has often sought a greater degree of artistic and directorial freedom but has found his dream elusive. "I am in some respects a victim of our times in the sense that I have a family, I have obligations, I have to take work. I have to do things that I don't particularly want to do because I have to pay monthly bills. There are stories I very much want to do when I have time to do them and can get someone interested in financing them." Arnold has made a great effort over the years to launch himself as an independent producer but though he came close quite a few times he has always had trouble with financing. He announced the formation of Arnold Productions in *Variety* as early as 1961 and put a lot of work into developing a number of projects, foremost of which is without doubt *A Circle of Wheels*.

A Circle of Wheels began as a stage play by Arthur Ross (one of the writers on *Creature from the Black Lagoon*) that got rave reviews when it opened in Los Angeles. Arnold saw it and was fascinated by its cinematic possibilties—it was both science-fiction and comedy. Arnold worked on developing and financing *A Circle of Wheels* off and on for about twenty years. A screenplay and budget was prepared and submitted to potential backers, but he was somehow unable to convey his vision to them. Part of the problem is that the story is truly offbeat and doesn't come close to fitting established genres. *A Circle of Wheels* represents, perhaps more than any other project, the kind of story Arnold would like to tell if he had the opportunity. It is worth our while to take a closer look and see what it is that attracted him.

Truth is framed in fantasy in this bizarre tale that delightfully takes up where Capek's *R.U.R.* left off.* Raymond and Elsie Shaw are a nice average husband and wife trapped in the banalities of upper

---

An outline for the screenplay of A Circle of Wheels *is given in Appendix 2.*

suburbia. Ray is an electronics engineer who has become a junior executive with professional problems and jealousies. His wife is a fussy homemaker too involved in her small son and hectic domestic routine to notice the lack of intimacy in their marriage. Their world turns upside down when a visit to the doctor reveals that they are growing little cogwheels in their livers. At first Ray revels in the idea that he is becoming a machine. Elsie's reaction is a soul-searching examination of her conscience. She thinks she must be paying for having premarital relations with Ray. Ray, meanwhile, attempts escape in an illicit affair but finds it useless. As their condition worsens they develop magnetic charges in their bodies that cause them alternately to attract and repel each other, and wreak havoc with all manner of machines they come in contact with. Life becomes so unbearable they attempt suicide, the preparations for which strike a shrewd, mischievous blend of the ludicrous and the macabre. This provides the catharsis that breaks them through to their essential humanity, and their cogwheels disappear.

A Circle of Wheels deals equally with the threatened mechanization of humanity and the more shadowed depths of modern secular conjugal love. The symbolism could be grim, pretentious, and dull, but the script displays a wit that reveals itself in the sharpness of its observation. The probing of sex relations is by turns tender and irascible, hilarious and gently grave, innocent and healthily ribald — often all at once. The dialogue has an admirable leanness, sureness, and tensile strength about it. The script is structured in a succession of swift, brief, perfectly cumulative scenes.

Anyone who might be tempted to dismiss Jack Arnold as a purely mercenary craftsman should reflect that while he spent years supporting his family with undistinguished television assignments, he continually struggled to bring *A Circle of Wheels* to the screen. In a letter to a potential backer he wrote, "My enthusiasm for this project is very high: One, it is unique and different; two, it is comedic and has boundless exploitation possibilities. A story dealing with the mores of our society, the mechanization of our lives carried to a reality beyond reality. In answer to your question about whether it can be 'brought off,' enclosed are some of the reviews the play received." Privately Arnold said, "I knew I could make a hell of a film out of the script, but I couldn't find a way to make the idea appealing to investors."

Another fantastic project that Arnold worked on was his own

Jack Arnold making a cameo appearance in John Landis' 1984 thriller Into the Night.

original science-fiction story tentatively titled *The Feathered Serpent* or *The Fifth Coming*. Before the dawn of history the ancient Atlanteans laid waste the Earth with their super-weapons. Survivors built a society in great caverns underground, emerging from time to time in strange spaceships now known as UFOs. As life reevolved on the Earth's surface they no longer had immunity to the new microorganisms there. The suits they wore to protect themselves gave them an awesome appearance, and they became part of the mythologies of ancient peoples like the Maya. A skeptical newsman expecting a hoax or mass hysteria discovers that the UFOs are all too real when he is abducted and flown through an active volcano to the Atlantean underworld. We follow him into a world where the elder scientists and their computers rule absolutely and are planning to enslave the upper world as well. He falls in love with a young Atlantean female, and the two of them become trapped in the struggle between the young Atlanteans and their tyrannical elders. They are exiled with the failed revolutionaries to the dreaded cavern of the mutants. All hope for thwarting the elders plans' for conquest being lost, our hero contrives to escape to the surface in a stolen spacecraft with his lady. They escape through the volcano to a remote Pacific island but lose the craft in the process. For awhile they live happily in this tropical paradise, but the Atlantean lass succumbs to surface-world bacteria and dies. The former skeptic is left alone on the island with knowledge of the coming invasion—but knows that no one will believe *him*!

Arnold wrote one potential investor, "If you are interested in the project a screenplay can be written in about five weeks. The budget of course depends on the finished screenplay, but considering the special effects and sets I estimate a budget of approximately one-and-a-half to three million. *Star Wars* cost six million plus. I believe we can make just as effective a film for at least half the cost."

Arnold wanted to film another original science-fiction story, *The Other Side of the Moon*, which he developed with collaborator Gene Ayres. It opens with a starship hurtling out of control through space. It is drawn into the gravitational pull of an unknown planet and crash-lands in a vast primeval jungle. As the crew struggles to survive, they discover huge objects that they take to be remnants of a lost civilization. They are periodically inundated by torrents of water from a cloudless sky and are attacked by giant insects. They all die without ever discovering the secret of this bizarre planet. A giant hand reaches down to pick up their ship and we discover that it is the hand

Jack Arnold with stars and director of Into the Night, *while filming his cameo appearance. Left to right: Director John Landis, Jack Arnold, and the film's stars Michelle Pfeiffer and Jeff Goldblum.*

of a little child, and that they had landed in someone's back lawn. The giant ruins were kids' toys, the monsters ordinary insects, and the torrents of water from the garden sprinkler.

While the basic premise of *The Other Side of the Moon* is nothing new in the annals of science fiction, there is a certain boldness of conception in the idea that the audience might really be kept in suspense about the planet's secret to the very end. It should also be noted that the story is not intended as a mere one-liner and special effects exercise. Arnold's intent was to use the film's premise to explore the notion of alternative worlds, the idea that one's reality depends on one's perception and perspective. "What had been hell for the space travellers had been someone else's ordinary garden lawn. As in *The Incredible Shrinking Man* I wanted to create the atmosphere in which familiar things become objects of mystery and terror. But I couldn't sell it to any of the studios because they wanted a happy ending. They didn't like the idea of everyone dying at the end."

Arnold has read a lot of science-fiction over the years — starting with *Amazing Stories* in the 1930s — but has found few stories really suitable for filming.

At least not for the kind of films I want to make. I need stories that allow for the creation of atmosphere, whereas so many of today's stories read more like technical manuals. The stories of Robert Heinlein are a marvelous exception; he has a couple of stories I'd like to film. In *Universe* a huge starship becomes a world unto itself as it drifts through space. *Stranger in a Strange Land* is another great story, one I'd love to do. Columbia bought it but they don't know what to do with it. They spent a lot of money on rewrites but never licked the problem. But the answer is right there in Heinlein's book. All one needs to do is just dramatise what he wrote without trying to improve on it. Another plus is that it wouldn't require elaborate special effects. It would make a great movie and I'd love to get it away from Columbia.

The suspense thriller is another genre that has strong appeal for Arnold. Like science-fiction and horror, a good thriller depends on the creation of atmosphere to be effective. Arnold has had a number of thrillers in development and came close to getting some of them produced. *Glass Eye*, for example, is a tale of international intrigue to have been shot in Greece. *Zach* is about an agent investigating international industrial espionage. Arnold also did some research for a thriller with an occult angle based on the life of psychic Peter Hurkos. *Odds On*, a novel by John Lange, was adapted as a screenplay by Arnold, who actually got financing for the picture in the summer of 1974. By a cruel twist of fate, however, the film's backer died shortly after. Unrealized projects are nothing new in Hollywood, but it is interesting to note the type of project that appeals to Arnold, invariably a work of imagination, mystery, or suspense requiring the creation of atmosphere.

In the following paragraphs Jack Arnold offers some reflections on the art of filmmaking as he knows it:

There is an old axiom in show business: The theater is an actor's medium, the novel the writer's medium, and film the director's medium. As most axioms this is not entirely accurate, although there is more than an ounce of truth in this particular one.

Before I go any further let me say categorically: *First there is the word.* Without it the actor cannot act, the director cannot direct. But the words, the play, the story, the screenplay are brought to fruition in many ways. The finished product is primarily a collaboration between writer and director and in some instances a certain rare breed of creative producer.

In the play, when the curtain goes up, the actors control the

Jack Arnold behind the camera in the mid–1970s.

destiny of the play. No one can yell, "Cut . . . let's do it again." The playwright and director stand backstage, fingers crossed, hoping it comes out the way they put it in. Hence the theater axiom. The novel is truly the writer's medium. Except for the occasional intervention of the publishing house editor, the writer and his typewriter are the masters of their own destiny.

But with regard to the role of the film director, and the special role of the film director of science-fiction, film is truly the director's medium. Though the writer comes first, we create from the words of the script a magical suspension of reality by means of visual images—interpretive, creative, and personal. Every director approaches his work in his own special way. As a film-maker, I can only speak with authority about myself and my approach. I try to create an atmosphere because if you're going to make a film of imagination, a film in which you ask an audience to believe things that are bizarre, you have to make them believe it. You cannot do this with actors and story *alone*. You have to create the kind of atmosphere while shooting in which you suspend disbelief to the point that the audience won't say to themselves "that's impossible" or "ridiculous." I think that the only way you can get an audience to accept the impossible is to get them involved in an atmosphere, a mood—a feeling of what you are trying to do. That's how I made use of actual physical locations. I made them work for my story. That's why I like to shoot in the desert or ocean beaches, locations that will help me create an atmosphere. Most of *It Came from Outer Space* was shot in the desert. I looked for places in the desert that engulfed me in atmosphere and that is where I would shoot. So I actively sought out those kinds of things that would give me atmosphere. Even in building sets in the studio we tried to bring into the studio those things that with the art director would help me create the mood. And I was very careful in casting to get the right kind of actors who could give the right kind of performance and who would understand what I meant when I said play the scene in thus and thus a manner. So it was a happy marriage of concept and fullfill-ment.

The creation of mood is a combination of using locations, sets, actors and camera in such a way that all of it has unity of design. The cameraman must be a close collaborator in the creative adventure. The angles, the way in which a film is photo-graphed, are a critical element but must be used anonymously. The audience must not be aware of the technical use of the camera—crazy angles, over use of the zoom lens. Some of the younger directors seem to have fallen love with the zoom lens and use it like a trombone! If the audience is aware of what the camera is doing you are doing something wrong. The audience loses contact with the mood and story and starts looking for tricks. That, to my mind, destroys the mood and the film becomes self-conscious.

The director must think and feel *visually*. Also, a good director must have a moviola in his head. He must have the finished, completed film in his head from the very beginning. Unlike the theater, the curtain doesn't go up on act one, scene one and fall at the end of the play. Films are not shot in sequence. Because of the very nature of the art, because of the economic constraints under which films are made, scenes were shot in the order demanded by availability of sets, locations, and actors. You might start shooting with the last scene in the story or somewhere inbetween. Each shot is a mosaic piece that the director must keep in its proper perspective and order in his head, what comes before and what comes after it, how all the pieces fit together to make a completely unified story. To help me do this I sketch and draw my own storyboard—not as a blueprint to follow but as a guide and visualization of my ideas, a conception of what my scenes should look like. Besides, being essentially lazy, this makes me do my homework. This doesn't preclude the possibility of improvisation on the set, it just keeps the mosaic straight in my head. For a story like *The Incredible Shrinking Man*, where the effects were such an important aspect of the story, my storyboard was invaluable to those very talented people in the special effects department. Every department head would know exactly what I wanted and there would be no misunderstanding or lack of knowledge about what I am going to do. When I got to a scene they were prepared for me, they knew what I wanted and the effect I wanted to achieve. It was precise and economical. That was the only way I could make it for under a million dollars, I knew exactly what I wanted. This is where my background and training stood me in good stead.

In a program of fifty or sixty films a year at Universal, many of them were classified "B" which meant they had limited budgets and schedules. When we had to make those "B" pictures we didn't have enough money to really make them. We had a very short schedule, and we had to use our imagination because we didn't have money. We invented things, we did things out of desperation because we didn't have the time or money that the directors who had "A" pictures had, who had forty or fifty days to make a picture. I had to make a picture in ten days. Some of these pictures are very exciting. That tension is almost generated on the set because I told them, "Look we've got ten days to do this, we can't fool around a minute . . . you've got to be concentrated, you've got to do it, and we've got to shoot sixteen pages." I've often shot eight, nine, ten pages a day. I challenged them to do it. Those films were used as a training ground not only for actors but also for directors and producers. Sometimes amazing stuff came out of the "B" program. We had to get along with bits of wire and string or whatever and lots of imagination because we didn't have the money or the time the "A" movies got. So it was a challenge and most of us met that challenge and did far better work on those "Bs" than some of them did on the "A" pictures.

I almost never went past two takes in those pictures, because I rehearsed the scene with the camera. Because I move the camera a lot. . . . I rehearse with the camera, so by the time I'm

Jack Arnold meets the press in a Renaissance palace as chief guest of honor at the XXe Festival International de Cinema Fantastic de Sitges, October, 1987.

ready for a take, everybody knows what's going on. We'd rehearse until they got it.

They got excited one day, I heard the assistant called the production office, "He's got eight pages and it's four o'clock, he's never going to get done." So I went over and picked up the phone and said, "I bet you a hundred bucks I'm through at six o'clock and have got all eight pages." They said, "We aren't going to take your bet." I said, "Good, goodbye." I did it in one take, but it took me an hour to rehearse that take. I must have had eighteen or nineteen dolly moves in it. Everything was timed. The actors had to hit the mark when the camera hit the mark. If the actor was off, then the camera was off. But I rehearsed it. When I got ready to do a take, they knew what they were going to do, the actors and the camera people and the sound people. So I didn't have to worry about them, all I had to worry about was if we'd get it. And then we'd do it. And if there was a little mistake in it, I'd say, let's do it once more. And if there was a big mistake I would make two head close-ups to cover it so I could cut it, then go on to the next scene.

How I approach making a film is, first of all I demand, and try to get, as good a script as I can get. I have not been overly successful at this, but once I get the script, I break the script down into shooting order and try to get a feeling about it, where the high points and low points of the story are. Does the story drag? or does the story need tightening? or are these characters believeable? Would they say the things that the author puts in their mouths or would they say something else? *That* you do kind of subconsciously when you read it, so I read a script more than once. When I get the word to prepare, I talk to the art director and the set decorators and we talk about what look the film should have. If it's a period piece, what period, if it's a modern story, that takes place today, where does it take place today, so that it has the look and feel of the time that the story takes place. Then I sit down with the art director and I make rough sketches which I give to a sketch artist who cleans it up for me, because if I tried to do all the details, it would take me months to do a good storyboard. But I do the rough sketches.

With regard to the art director, his work starts with my work. The art director works under my supervision. He brings in plans and I will okay them or adjust them and say, look, I'll want this or I'd like that.

I've worked very closely with the editor on every film I've made because that's where you can either make or break a film. It's a law of the Directors' Guild that the director has the first cut. The editor will assemble the film and put it in sequence, then I'll sit down with him and we'll cut it—and usually it stays that way. Unless—and it's happened to me—you get a producer that thinks he knows more than he really knows.

It's no trick to spend twenty-two million dollars. The trick is to do something on a limited budget and get the same or better effects by using real talent and making your story and your atmosphere work for you rather than doing it by excess shooting or waiting for the cloud to be in the right place and shooting every scene from every angle with the idea that one of the angles has got to be good since you've covered it from every angle. But I never had that luxury, and I frankly wouldn't know how to do it, but I'd be bored to death doing it that way because *I* want to create the film. I don't want the editor to create the film, I want to create the film. I like the challenge.

The atmosphere and special effects in my films were done very well given the technique of the time. We didn't have the technique that was available to *Star Wars*. We didn't have the electronic gimmicks they could use nor the two years that Lucas spent doing the special effects or the millions of dollars he spent making the film. My films were usually under a million dollars. While they often made more money than the "A" films relative to what was spent on them, they were still classified as science-fiction "B" films. It was the audience that made them more than that—their reaction to the films. *Star Wars* is an exercise in the wonders of our electronic technique. The director shows his good taste but is essentially doing a cartoon, a comic strip in which good conquers evil, where everything is black-and-white. He sets it in a never-never land in another galaxy and the people are charming and the effects are wondrous and it's an upbeat story and the kids love it, I loved it. But it is hardly the kind of science-fiction that I consider important.

Whenever a science-fiction picture would come onto the lot they would assign it to me and I would do it with great pleasure. One of my fears as a person was that science was getting out of hand, beginning to do things that we would later regret, that we were developing weapons that would destroy us. And now they're fooling around with genes—God knows where they're going to go with that. This is evidence that what we were saying in the fifties and sixties is certainly coming true. I was sensitive to this, having lived through a war and having seen what destruction can do and seeing where we were going with the madness around us. I was happy to say anything I could to wake people up to the horrendous choices we have to make so that some of us might make the right choices. And hopefully enough of us would be aware of what is going on that we would exercise our rights.

Because the good science-fiction films like mine made money, suddenly AIP and others started making imitations of them but without class. They tried to imitate the formula but they left out the most important ingredient. What was the spine? What was the story you were trying to tell? Were you trying just to tell a story of monsters? Were you trying to have a moral? Were you trying to create an atmosphere? They had none. They made the Amazing Fifty-Foot Amazon or whatever, and then the Japanese began sending over giant monsters that were obvious rubber suits, The Beast That Ate Brooklyn, that sort of thing. The market was saturated with that kind of film, and the day came when you couldn't sell the studio a science-fiction story for gratis. So I left for England where I made *The Mouse That Roared* which is a kind of science-fiction comedy. A fantasy that still had something to say.

I don't go about directing a picture any differently than I go about telling a story. If I tell a story, it's a series of incidents tied together by the characters who people the story and each of them have different functions in the story. What I look for is believability, depending on what kind of a story it is. If it's a comedy, I look for fun, I look for where the comedy is and if the comedy is motivated or if it's just tacked on. Does it come out of the situation? Who would be the best actors to play it? If it's a drama, then does it ring true? Does it touch you? Am I touched by it? Do I feel for the people? Do I care about the people? Because if I don't care about the people, I don't expect anyone else to care about them. So, I think that the cardinal rule in making a story is to make sure that it's peopled by a cast that you care about or hate. But you must have some kind of emotional feeling toward them, otherwise if you are reading it as a book you don't even turn the page. You have to have something to make you turn the page, and you have to have something to make you sit in the theatre. If it's a two or two-and-a-half-hour film, you shouldn't feel like you've been sitting there for three days. I've seen films that have gone on for two-and-a-half hours and I thought I would never walk again. And I've seen films three hours long that were so well made I felt like I'd just sat down, I didn't want it to end.

So, everything that encompasses the art of telling a story is what I look for. And, if I'm a good storyteller, with the technique that I've learned over the years, I'll make a good film of it. It's a combination of telling a story, and technique, and of course casting and getting the right people to surround you.

I like all kinds of stories. There isn't a kind of story I don't like. I like science-fiction, I love comedy. I love *The Mouse That Roared*—it's my favorite picture, and it's a comedy—I think almost as much of *The Incredible Shrinking Man*, which is science-fiction. I don't have a favorite subject. The only preference I have is a good script. I don't put films in compartments. Some films I'm proud of, some films I'm not so proud of—but I consider myself a storyteller. I can tell any kind of story, and if it's a good story it will be a good film. It's not like being a doctor specializing in ear, nose, and throat and the rest of the body can go to hell. I feel more like an old general practitioner who takes care of the whole body when you're sick—and makes house calls too!

Jack Arnold sees himself primarily as a storyteller. It doesn't matter if the story is simple kid-stuff or has been told a few times

Jack Arnold in the 1980s.

before; it is the telling that matters, how it is told. If we do not find his films to be deeply personal statements, we may nonetheless detect the presence of the guiding intelligence of the storyteller. One has a definite feeling that there is a personality behind his films who is delighted to be telling us a story. We may not find much in the way of recurrent themes, but we can at least admire his virtuosity. Moreover, Arnold is remarkably skilled and often brilliant. He is never asleep at the wheel and always knows exactly what he wants. Not that every idea is always great, but there are good ideas in every film. In general, his films show respect for the subject matter (regardless of genre), characters, and audience expectations. This reflects Arnold's deep respect for the motion picture medium and himself, qualities rare enough in the commercial cinema of today.

Since his "discovery" in the early seventies by British critic John Baxter and French critic Jean-Marie Sabatier, Arnold has enjoyed an increasing reputation, especially in Europe. In July 1975 he was asked to be the master of ceremonies at the XIII Festival Internazione de film di fantascienza, where he was honored with a retrospective of several of his best films. The printed program hailed him as "... probably the last of that special breed of film makers who managed to make personal films from subjects he himself did not originate ... one of the few film *auteurs* in a genre which all too often places more emphasis on the scenario writer or special effects creator than on the director." He received additional attention from festivals in Tucson and Rio de Janeiro, and made a personal appearance in 1981 at the Mill Valley Film Festival (outside San Francisco) for a screening of *The Incredible Shrinking Man*. The program described him as "... a person of such versatility, talent, and integrity that he is able to transcend the Hollywood preoccupation with box office success, ignore the formulas for such success, and yet succeed by the sheer weight of his talent and person ... who in more than thirty years of film making has proven that there is no budget so limited, no shooting time so short, no cast so unknown, and no screenplay so obscure that it cannot be turned into a work of art, intelligence and technical finesse—and succeed financially." In January 1982 he was a special guest at the Seattle Science Fiction Xpo. The same year Arnold appeared in a lengthy interview in the prestigious *Cahiers du Cinema*. In 1983–84 WDR/West German Television ran a special series on Arnold including screenings of all of his science-fiction pictures and *The Glass Web* with added background and interview material. Most recently he was chief guest of honor at the XXe Festival International de Cinema Fantastic de Sitges (Spain) in October of 1987.

The reason for the tardiness of this recognition is not difficult to uncover. It is the generation born after World War II that has been most affected by Arnold's films. Until this generation reached its majority, the films of Jack Arnold were taken utterly for granted.

My films from the fifties and sixties have caught on with the younger generation which is personally something that gives me great joy. I didn't instigate this other than I happened to have made those films. I think the young people are seeing in those films what I was trying to say—even sharper than the generation that saw those films when they were made. The young people today are much more attuned to the mores of our society and the subtleties of our society and they see in those science-fiction films exactly the points I was trying to make. It gives me tremendous joy that so many young people admire those films and are fans of mine. I appreciate them deeply.

Those who are in some way moved by the films of Jack Arnold may wish to know his films better and see to the perpetuation of what is best in his work. It is hoped that the preceding chapters will both contribute to a revival of Arnold's best films and encourage new filmmakers in the art of strong, straightforward storytelling.

Filmography

Short Subjects*

For Promotional Films, Inc., 1947–49.
Chicken of Tomorrow, U.S. Dept. of Agriculture.
Beachwood Package Home, John Wannamaker.
Fundraising film for the Jewish Consumptive Relief Society.
Commercials for Weathervane Suits.
Commercials for Lampell Suits.
Promotional film for Local 91, I.L.G.W.U.
The Road, Jewish Anti-Defamation League.

In 1968 Arnold made a short at MGM for the Treasury Department promoting the sale of savings bonds.

Theatrical Features

With These Hands. International Ladies Garment Workers Union Production. *Producers,* Jack Arnold, Lee Goodman; *director,* Jack Arnold; *screenplay,* Morton Wishengrad; *photography,* Gerald Hirschfeld; *music composed and conducted by* Morris Mamorsky; *editor,* Charles R. Senf. *Running time:* 52 minutes. B & W. *Release:* August 1950. **Cast:** *Alexander Brody,* Sam Levene; *Jenny,* Arlene Francis; *DeLeo,* Joseph Wiseman; *Boss,* Louis Sorin; *Doctor,* Alexander Scorby; *Business Agent,* Rudy Bond; *Doctor (in 1913),* Alexander Lockwood; *Impartial Chairman,* Haskell Coffin; *Triangle Boss,* Julius Bing; *"Bagel and Lox,"* Morris Strassberg; *Typist,* Rolly Bester; *Girl in Fire,* Gail Gregg; *Tess,* Judy Walther.

Girls in the Night. Universal-International. *Producer,* Albert J. Cohen; *director,* Jack Arnold; *story, screenplay,* Ray Buffum; *photography,* Carl Guthrie; *art direction,* Alexander Golitzen, Robert Boyle; *musical direction,* Joesph Gershenson; *sound,* Leslie I. Carey, Robert Pritchard; *editor,* Paul Weatherwax; *dance number staged by* Hal Belfer. *Running time:* 82 minutes. B & W. *Release:* January 1953. **Cast:** *Georgia,* Joyce Holden; *Chuck Haynes,* Harvey Lembeck; *Joe*

*This list is not exhaustive.

213

Spurgeon, Leonard Freeman; *Vera Schroeder,* Jaclynne Greene; *Irv Kelleher,* Don Gordon; *Hannah Haynes,* Patricia Hardy; *Alice Haynes,* Glenda Farrell; *Charlie Haynes,* Anthony Ross; *Kovacs,* Emile Meyer; *Hilda Haynes,* Susan Odin; *Angela,* Valerie Jackson; *McGinty,* Charles Cane; *Frankie,* Tommie Farrell; *Judge,* John Eldredge; *Blind Mimosa,* Paul E. Burns.

It Came from Outer Space. Universal-International. *Producer,* William Alland; *director,* Jack Arnold; *screenplay,* Harry Essex; *story,* Ray Bradbury; *camera,* Clifford Stine; *art director,* Bernard Herzbrun, Robert Boyle; *musical direction,* Joseph Gershenson; *editor,* Paul Weatherwax; *special photography,* David Horsley. *Running time:* 80 minutes. 3-D, B & W. *Release:* May 1953. **Cast:** *John Putnam,* Richard Carlson; *Ellen Fields,* Barbara Rush; *Sheriff Matt Warren,* Charles Drake; *George,* Russel Johnson; *Frank Daylon,* Joseph Sawyer; *Dave Loring,* Alan Dexter; *Pete Davis,* Dave Willock; *Dr. Snell,* George Eldridge; *Dr. Snell's Assistant,* Brad Jackson; *Toby,* Warren McGregor; *Tom,* George Selk; *Sam,* Edgar Dearing; *Jane,* Kathleen Hughes; *Deputy Reed,* William Pullen; *Mrs. Frank Daylon,* Virginia Mullen; *Dugan,* Robert S. Carson; *Lober,* Dick Pinner; *Man,* Ned Davenport; *Perry,* Witey Haupt.

The Glass Web. Universal-International. *Producer,* Albert J. Cohen; *director,* Jack Arnold; *screenplay,* Robert Blees, Leonard Lee; *based on a novel by* Max Simon Ehrlich; *photography,* Maury Gertsman; *art direction,* Bernard Herzbrun, Eric Orbom; *musical direction,* Joseph Gershenson; *sound,* Leslie I. Carey, Robert Pritchard; *editor,* Ted J. Kent. *Running time:* 81 minutes. 3-D, B & W. *Release:* October 1953. **Cast:** *Henry Hayes,* Edward G. Robinson; *Don Newell,* John Forsythe; *Louise Newell,* Marcia Henderson; *Paula,* Kathleen Hughes; *Dave Markson,* Richard Denning; *Stevens,* Hugh Sanders; *Sonia,* Jean Willes; *Jake,* Henry O. Tyler; *Bob Warren,* Clark Howat; *Other Man,* Paul Dubov; *Announcer,* John Hiestand; *Plainclothesman,* Bob Nelson; *Everett,* Dick Stewart; *Barbara Newell,* Jeri Lon James; *Jimmy Newell,* Duncan Richardson.

Creature from the Black Lagoon. Universal-International. *Producer,* William Alland; *director,* Jack Arnold; *underwater scenes directed by* James C. Havens; *screenplay,* Harry Essex, Arthur Ross; *story,* Maurice Zimm; *photography,* William E. Snyder; *special photography,* Charles S. Welbourne; *art direction,* Bernard Herzbrun, Hilyard Brown; *musical direction,* Joseph Gershenson; *sound,* Leslie I. Carey, Joe Lapis; *editor,* Ted J. Kent. *Running time:* 79 minutes. 3-D, B & W. *Release:* February 1954. **Cast:** *David Reed,* Richard Carlson; *Kay,* Julia Adams; *Mark Williams,* Richard Denning; *Carl Maia,* Antonio Moreno; *Lucas,* Nestor Paiva; *Dr. Thompson,* Whit Bissell; *Zee,* Bernie Gozier; *Louis,* Rod Redwing; *Chico,* Henry Escalante; *Thomas,* Julio Lopez; *Gill Man (in water),* Ricou Browning; *Gill Man (on land),* Ben Chapman; *Dr. Matos,* Sydney Mason.

Revenge of the Creature. Universal-International. *Producer,* William Alland; *director,* Jack Arnold; *screenplay,* Martin Berkeley; *story,* William Alland; *photography,* Charles S. Welbourne; *art director,* Alexander Golitzen, Alfred Sweeney; *music,* Joseph Gershenson; *sound,* Leslie I. Carey, Jack Bolger; *editor,* Paul Weatherwax. *Running time:* 82 minutes. 3-D, B & W. *Release:* March 1955. **Cast:** *Prof. Clete Furguson,* John Agar; *Helen Dobson,* Lori Nelson; *Joe Hayes,* John Bromfield; *Lucas,* Nestor Paiva; *Jackson Foster,* Grandon Rhodes; *Lou*

Gibson, Dave Willock; *George Johnson*, Robert B. Williams; *Captain of Police*, Charles Cane; *Pete*, Brett Halsey; *Jennings*, Clint Eastwood.

The Man from Bitter Ridge. Universal-International. *Producer*, Howard Pine; *director*, Jack Arnold; *screenplay*, Lawrence Roman; *adaptation*, Teddi Sherman; *based on a novel by* William MacLeod Raine; *photography*, Russell Metly; *art direction*, Alexander Golitzen, Bill Newberry; *music*, Joseph Gershenson; *sound*, Leslie I. Carey, Robert Pritchard; *editor*, Milton Carruth. *Running time:* 80 minutes. Eastman Color. *Release:* April 1955. **Cast:** *Jeff Carr*, Lex Barker; *Holly Kenton*, Mara Corday; *Alec Black*, Stephen McNally; *Ranse Jackman*, John Dehner; *Shep Bascom*, Ray Teal; *Walter Dunham*, Trevor Bardette; *Lino Jackman*, Warren Stevens; *Clem*, Myron Healey; *Norman Roberts*, John Harmon; *Jace Gordon*, Richard Garland; *Wolf Landers*, John Cliff; *Hank Mains*, Jennings Miles.

Tarantula! Universal-International. *Producer*, William Alland; *director*, Jack Arnold; *screenplay*, Robert M. Fresco, Martin Berkeley; *story*, Jack Arnold, Robert M. Fresco; *photography*, George Robinson; *art direction*, Alexander Golitzen, Alfred Sweeney; *music supervision*, Joseph Gershenson; *sound*, Leslie I. Carey, Frank Wilkinson; *editor*, William M. Morgan. *Running time:* 80 minutes. B & W. *Release:* November 1955. **Cast:** *Dr. Matt Hastings*, John Agar; *Stephanie "Steve" Clayton*, Mara Corday; *Prof. Gerald Deemer*, Leo G. Carroll; *Sheriff Jack Andrews*, Nestor Paiva; *Joe Burch*, Ross Elliott; *Lt. John Nolan*, Ed Rand; *Townsend*, Raymond Bailey; *First Pilot*, Clint Eastwood.

Red Sundown. Universal-International. *Producer*, Albert Zugsmith; *director*, Jack Arnold; *screenplay*, Martin Berkeley; *story*, Lewis B. Patten; *photography*, William Snyder; *technicolor consultant*, William Frtizsche; *art direction*, Alexander Golitzen, Eric Orbom; *music*, Joseph Gershenson; *song, "Red Sundown" written and sung by* Terry Gilkyson; *sound*, Leslie I. Carey, Corson Jowett; *editor*, Edward Curtiss. *Running time:* 82 minutes. Technicolor. *Release:* January 1956. **Cast:** *Alec Longmire*, Rory Calhoun; *Caroline Murphy*, Martha Hyer; *Jade Murphy*, Dean Jagger; *Rufus Henshaw*, Robert Middleton; *Purvis*, James Millican; *Sam Baldwin*, Trevor Bardette; *Maria*, Lita Baron; *Chet Swann*, Grant Williams; *Rod Zellman*, Leo Gordon; *Hughie Clore*, David Kasday; *Chuck Webb*, Stevie Wootton; *Bert Flynn*, Steve Darrell; *First Zellman Henchman*, John Carpenter; *Second Zellman Henchman*, Alex Sharp; *Third Zellman Henchman*, Henry Wills; *Jed*, Donald Kerr.

Outside the Law. Universal-International. *Producer*, Albert J. Cohen; *director*, Jack Arnold; *screenplay*, Danny Arnold; *story*, Peter R. Brooke; *photography*, Irving Glassberg; *art direction*, Alexander Golitzen, Eric Orbom; *set decorators*, Russell A. Gausman, Oliver Emert; *music supervision*, Milton Rosen; *costumes*, Rosemary Odell; *sound*, Leslie I. Carey, James Thomson; *editor*, Irving Birnbaum. *Running time:* 82 minutes. B & W. *Release:* April 1956. **Cast:** *Johnny Salvo*, Ray Danton; *Maria Craven*, Leigh Snowdon; *Don Kastner*, Grant Williams; *Alec Conrad*, Onslow Stevens; *Maury Saxon*, Judson Pratt; *Phil Schwartz*, Jack Kruschen; *Phillip Bormann*, Raymond Bailey; *Harris*, Floyd Simmons; *Milo Barker*, Mel Welles; *Parker*, Arthur Hanson; *Bill McReady*, Jesse Kirkpatrick; *Redding*, Vernon Rich; *Clinton*, Dan Sturkie.

The Incredible Shrinking Man. Universal-International. *Producer*, Albert Zugsmith; *director*, Jack Arnold; *novel, screenplay*, Richard Matheson;

photography, Ellis W. Carter; *special photography*, Clifford Stine; *art direction*, Alexander Golitzen, Robert Clatworthy; *set decoration*, Russell A. Gausman, Ruby R. Levitt; *music supervision*, Joseph Gershenson; *sound*, Leslie I. Carey, Robert Pritchard; *editor*, Al Joseph. *Running time:* 81 minutes. B & W. *Release:* February 1957. **Cast:** *Scott Carey*, Grant Williams; *Louise Carey*, Randy Stuart; *Clarice*, April Kent; *Charlie Carey*, Paul Langton; *Dr. Thomas Silver*, Raymond Bailey; *Dr. Arthur Bramson*, William Schallert; *Barker*, Frank Scannell; *Nurse*, Helene Marshall; *Nurse*, Diana Darrin; *Small Man*, Billy Curtis; *TV Commentator*, John Hiestand; *Giant*, Lockhart Martin; *bit*, Joe La Barba; *bit*, Reg Parton.

The Tattered Dress. Universal-International. *Producer*, Albert Zugsmith; *director*, Jack Arnold; *screenplay*, George Zuckerman; *photography*, Carl E. Guthrie; *art direction*, Alexander Golitzen, Bill Newberry; *set decoration*, Russell A. Gausman, John P. Austin; *music*, Frank Skinner; *music supervision*, Joseph Gershenson; *sound*, Leslie I. Carey, Robert Pritchard; *editor*, Edward Curtiss. *Running time:* 93 minutes. CinemaScope, Technicolor. *Release:* February 1957. **Cast:** *James Gordon Blane*, Jeff Chandler; *Diane Blane*, Jeanne Crain; *Nick Hoak*, Jack Carson; *Carol Morrow*, Gail Russell; *Charleen Reston*, Elaine Stewart; *Billy Giles*, George Tobias; *Lester Rawlings*, Edward Andrews; *Michael Reston*, Philip Reed; *Ralph Adams*, Edward C. Platt; *Frank Mitchell*, Paul Birch; *Paul Vernon*, Alexander Lockwood; *Judge*, Edwin Jerome; *Court Clerk*, William Schallert; *Second Jury Foreman*, Joseph Granby; *Cal Morrison*, Frank Scannell.

Man in the Shadow. Universal-International. *Producer*, Albert Zugsmith; *director*, Jack Arnold; *screenplay*, Gene L. Coon; *photography*, Arthur E. Arling; *art direction*, Alexander Golitzen, Alfred Sweeney; *set decoration*, Russell A. Gausman, John P. Austin; *music supervision*, Joseph Gershenson; *sound*, Leslie I. Carey, Joe Lapis; *editor*, Edward Curtiss. *Running time:* 80 minutes. CinemaScope, B & W. *Release:* November 1957. **Cast:** *Ben Sadler*, Jeff Chandler; *Virgil Renchler*, Orson Welles; *Skippy Renchler*, Colleen Miller; *Ab Begley*, Ben Alexander; *Helen Sadler*, Barbara Lawrence; *Ed Yates*, John Larch; *Hank James*, James Gleason; *Aiken Clay*, Royal Dano; *Herb Parker*, Paul Fix; *Chet Huneker*, Leo Gordon; *Jesus Cisrenos*, Martin Garralaga; *Tony Santoro*, Mario Siletti; *Len Bookman*, Charles Horvath; *Jim Shaney*, William Schallert; *Harry Youngquist*, Joseph J. Green; *Jake Kelly*, Forrest Lewis; *Dr. Creighton*, Harry Harvey, Sr.; *Juan Martin*, Joe Schneider; *Gateman*, Mort Mills.

The Lady Takes a Flyer. Universal-International. *Producer*, William Alland; *director*, Jack Arnold; *screenplay*, Danny Arnold; *story*, Edmund H. North; *photography*, Irving Glassberg; *art direction*, Alexander Golitzen, Richard H. Riedel; *set decoration*, Russell A. Gausman, Oliver Emert; *music*, Herman Stein; *music supervision*, Joseph Gershenson; *sound*, Leslie I. Carey, Corson Jowett; *editor*, Sherman Todd. *Running time:* 95 minutes. CinemaScope; Eastman Color. *Release:* January 1958. **Cast:** *Maggie Colby*, Lana Turner; *Mike Dandridge*, Jeff Chandler; *Al Reynolds*, Richard Denning; *Nikki Taylor*, Andra Martin; *Phil Donahue*, Chuck Connors; *Nurse Kennedy*, Reta Shaw; *Frank Henshaw*, Alan Hale, Jr.; *Willie Ridgley*, Jerry Paris; *Collie Minor*, Dee J. Thompson; *Childreth*, Nestor Paiva; *Tower Officer*, James Doherty.

High School Confidential! MGM. *Producer*, Albert Zugsmith; *director*, Jack Arnold; *screenplay*, Lewis Meltzer, Robert Blees; *screen story*, Robert Blees;

photography, Harold J. Marzonati; *art direction,* William A. Horning, Hans Peters; *set decoration,* Henry Grace, Arthur Krams; *song: "High School Confidential!"* by Jerry Lee Lewis, Ron Hargrave; *sung by* Lewis; *sound,* Dr. Wesley C. Miller; *editor,* Ben Lewis. *Running time:* 85 minutes. CinemaScope, B & W. *Release:* May 1958. **Cast:** *Tony Baker/Mike Wilson,* Russ Tamblyn; *Arlene Williams,* Jan Sterling; *J.I. Coleridge,* John Drew Barrymore; *Gwen Dulaine,* Mamie Van Doren; *Joan Staples,* Diane Jergens; *Himself,* Jerry Lee Lewis; *Bix,* Ray Anthony; *Mr. A,* Jackie Coogan; *Quinn,* Charles Chaplin, Jr.; *Jukey Judlow,* Burt Douglas; *Steve Bentley,* Michael Landon; *Doris,* Jody Fair; *Poetess,* Phillipa Fallon; *Kitty,* Robin Raymond; *Jack Staples,* James Todd; *William Remington Kane,* Lyle Talbot; *Wheeler-Dealer,* William Wellman, Jr.; *Henchman,* Texas Joe Foster; *Gloria,* Diana Darrin; *Petey,* Carl Thayler; *Morino,* Irwin Berke.

The Space Children. Paramount. *Producer,* William Alland; *director,* Jack Arnold; *screenplay,* Bernard C. Schoenfeld; *from a story by* Tom Filer; *photography,* Ernest Laszlo; *special photographic effects,* John P. Fulton; *art direction,* Hal Pereira, Roland Anderson; *set decoration,* Sam Comer, Frank McKelvy; *music score,* Van Cleave; *sound,* Philip Wisdom, Charles Grenzbach; *film editor,* Terry Morse. *Running time:* 69 minutes. B & W. *Release:* June 1958. **Cast:** *Bud Brewster,* Michel Ray; *Dave Brewster,* Adam Williams; *Ann Brewster,* Peggy Webber; *Tim,* John Washbrook; *Hank,* Jackie Coogan; *Colonel Manley,* Richard Shannon; *Dr. Wahrman,* Raymond Bailey; *Eadie,* Sandy Descher; *Major Thomas,* Larry Pennell; *Mr. James,* Peter Baldwin; *Sentry,* Ty Hungerford; *Joe,* Russell D. Johnson; *Saul Wahrman,* David Bair; *Ken Brewster,* Johnny Crawford; *Phyllis,* Eilene Janssen; *Peg,* Jean Engstrom; *Frieda Johnson,* Vera Marshe.

Monster on the Campus. Universal-International. *Producer,* Joseph Gershenson; *director,* Jack Arnold; *screenplay,* David Ducan; *photography,* Russell Metty; *special photography,* Clifford Stine; *art direction,* Alexander Golitzen; *set decoration,* Russell A. Gausman, Julia Heron; *sound,* Leslie I. Carey, Joe Lapis; *editor,* Ted J. Kent. *Running time:* 76 minutes. B & W. *Release:* October 1958. **Cast:** *Dr. Donald Blake,* Arthur Franz; *Madeline Howard,* Joanna Moore; *Lt. Mike Stevens,* Judson Pratt; *Molly Riordan,* Helen Westcott; *Gilbert Howard,* Alexander Lockwood; *Jimmy Flanders,* Troy Donahue; *Sylvia Lockwood,* Nancy Walters; *Sgt. Powell,* Phil Harvey; *Dr. Oliver Cole,* Whit Bissell; *Sgt. Eddie Daniels,* Ross Elliott.

No Name on the Bullet. Universal-International. *Producers,* Howard Christie, Jack Arnold; *director,* Jack Arnold; *screenplay,* Gene L. Coon; *from a story by* Howard Amacker; *photography,* Harold Lipstein; *art direction,* Alexander Golitzen, Robert E. Smith; *set decoration,* Russell A. Gausman, Theodore Driscoll; *music,* Herman Stein; *music supervision,* Joseph Gershenson; *sound,* Leslie I. Carey, Frank Wilkinson; *editor,* Frank Gross. *Running time:* 77 minutes. CinemaScope, Eastman Color. *Release:* February 1959. **Cast:** *John Gant,* Audie Murphy; *Anne Benson,* Joan Evans; *Luke Canfield,* Charles Drake; *Roseanne Fraden,* Virginia Grey; *Fraden,* Warren Stevens; *Asa Canfield,* R.G. Armstrong; *Buck Hastings,* Willis Bouchey; *Judge Benson,* Edgar Stehli; *Sid,* Charles Watts; *Stricker,* Karl Swenson; *Harold Miller,* Jerry Paris; *Pierce,* Whit Bissell; *Chaffee,* John Alderson; *Reeger,* Simon Scott; *Storekeeper,* Russ Bender; *Hugo Mott,* Jim Hyland; *Chief Teller,* Herold Goodwin; *Branch,* Willard Willingham.

The Mouse That Roared. Columbia. *Producer,* Walter Shenson; *associate producer,* Jon Penington; *director,* Jack Arnold; *screenplay,* Roger MacDougall, Stanley Mann; *from the novel by* Leonard Wibberley; *photography,* John Wilcox; *art direction,* Geoffrey Drake; *title design,* Maurice Binder; *music,* Edwin Astley; *sound,* Richard Marden, Red Law, George Stephenson; *production supervisor,* Leon Becker; *production manager,* James Ware; *editor,* Raymond Poulton. *Running time:* 83 minutes. Eastman Color by Pathé, England. *Release:* October 1959. **Cast:** *Tully/Gloriana/Montjoy,* Peter Sellers; *Helen,* Jean Seberg; *Will,* William Hartnell; *Kokintz,* David Kossoff; *Benter,* Leo McKern; *Snippet,* MacDonald Parke; *U.S. Secretary of Defense,* Austin Willis; *Roger,* Timothy Bateson; *Cobbley,* Monty Landis; *BBC Announcer,* Colin Gordon; *Pedro,* Harold Kashet; *O'Hara,* George Margo; *Mulligan,* Richard Gatehouse; *Ticket Collector,* James Cey; *Cunard Captain,* Stuart Sanders; *Cunard 2nd Officer,* Ken Stanley; *Army Captain,* Bill Edwards.

Bachelor in Paradise. MGM. *Producer,* Ted Richmond; *director,* Jack Arnold; *screenplay,* Valentine Davies, Hal Kanter; *story,* Vera Caspary; *photography,* Joseph Ruttenberg; *art direction,* George W. Davis, Hans Peters; *set decoration,* Henry Grace, Keogh Gleason; *music,* Henry Mancini; *sound,* Milton Franklin; *editor,* Richard W. Farrell; *assistant director,* Eric von Stroheim, Jr. *Running time:* 108 minutes. CinemaScope, Metrocolor. *Release:* October 1961. **Cast:** *Adam J. Niles,* Bob Hope; *Rosemary Howard,* Lana Turner; *Dolores Jynson,* Janis Paige; *Larry Delavane,* Jim Hutton; *Linda Delavane,* Paula Prentiss; *Thomas W. Jynson,* Don Porter; *Camille Quinlaw,* Virginia Grey; *Judge Peterson,* Agnes Moorehead; *Mrs. Pickering,* Florence Sundberg; *Rodney Jones,* Clinton Sundberg; *Austin Palfrey,* John McGiver; *Backett,* Alan Hewitt; *Mrs. Brown,* Reta Shaw.

A Global Affair. MGM. *Producer,* Hall Bartlett; *director,* Jack Arnold; *screenplay,* Arthur Marx, Bob Fisher, Charles Lederer; *story,* Eugene Vale; *photography,* Joseph Ruttenberg; *art direction,* George W. Davis, Preston Ames; *set decoration,* Charles Thompson; *music,* Dominic Frontiere; *sound,* Milton Franklin; *editor,* Bud Molin; *assistant director,* Tom Shaw, Lee Lukather; *associate producer,* Eugene Vale; *executive producer,* Bernard Schwartz. *Running time:* 84 minutes. B & W . *Release:* January 1964. **Cast:** *Frank Larrimore,* Bob Hope; *Sonya Ublenko,* Lilo Pulver; *Lisette Varine,* Michele Mercier; *Yvette,* Elga Anderson; *Dolores,* Yvonne DeCarlo; *Randy,* Robert Sterling; *Fumiko,* Miiko Taka; *Mr. Snifter,* John McGiver; *Under Secretary Segura,* Nehemiah Persoff; *Dugan,* Mickey Shaughnessy; *Guy Duval,* Jacques Bergerac; *Baby Monroe,* Denise & Danielle Monroe; *Himself,* Hugh Downs; *Nigerian Representative,* Robes Johnson; *Jean Baker,* Georgia Hayes; *Wayland,* Edmond Ryan; *Cab Driver,* William Halop; *Miss Argyll,* Reta Shaw; *Chiquita,* Inez Pedroza; *Madelaine,* Francoise Ruggerio; *Sigrid,* Barbara Bouchette; *Judge,* Voltaire Perkins.

The Lively Set. Universal. *Producer,* William Alland; *director,* Jack Arnold; *screenplay,* Mel Goldberg, William Wood; *story,* William Alland, Mel Goldberg; *photography,* Carl Guthrie; *art direction,* Alexander Golitzen, Walter Simonds; *set decoration,* John McCarthy, Joe Kish; *music,* Bobby Darin; *sound,* Waldon O. Watson, Josh Westmoreland; *editor,* Archie Marshek; *assistant director,* James Welch. *Running Time:* 95 minutes. Color. *Release:* August 1964. **Cast:** *Casey,* James Darren; *Eadie,* Pamela Tiffin; *Chuck,* Doug McClure; *Doreen,* Joanie Sommers; *Marge,* Marilyn Maxwell; *Paul Manning,* Charles Drake; *Stanford Rogers*

Peter Mann; *Mona*, Carole Wells; *Ernie*, Ross Elliott; *Moody*, Russ Conway; *As themselves:* Mickey Thompson, James Nelson, Dave MacDonald, Duane Carter, Billy Krause, Ron Miller, George Stecher; *Celeste*, Frances Robinson; *Prof. Collins*, Martin Blaine; *Himself*, Max Schumacher; *Himself*, Dick Whittinghill; *Policeman*, Greg Morris; *TV Announcer*, Tom Kelly; *Club M. C.*, Wink Martindale.

Hello Down There. Ivan Tors–Paramount. *Producer*, George Sherman; *director*, Jack Arnold; *screenplay*, John McGreevey, Frank Telford; *story by* Ivan Tors, Art Arthur; *photography*, Clifford Poland; *art director*, Jack Collis; *set decorator*, Don Ivey; *music*, Jeff Barry; *sound effects editor*, Leonard Davison; *film editor*, Erwin Dumbrille; *assistant director/assistant producer*, William C. Gerrity; *underwater sequences directed by* Ricou Browning; *photographed by* Lamar Boren, Jordan Klein. *Running time:* 98 minutes. Color. *Release:* March 1969. **Cast:** *Fred Miller*, Tony Randall; *Vivian Miller*, Janet Leigh; *Nate Ashbury*, Roddy McDowall; *T.R. Hollister*, Jim Backus; *Mel Cheever*, Ken Berry; *Myrtle Ruth*, Charlotte Rae; *Lorrie Miller*, Kay Cole; *Harold Webster*, Richard Dreyfuss; *Marvin Webster*, Lou Wagner; *Tommie Miller*, Gary Tigerman; *Jonah*, Arnold Stang; *Sonarman*, Harvey Lembeck; *Himself*, Merv Griffin; *Dr. Wells*, Lee Meredith; *Admiral Sheridan*, Bruce Gordon; *Alan Briggs*, Frank Schuller; *Mrs. Webster*, Henny Backus; *Reilly*, Pat Henning; *Philo*, Jay Laskay; *Mr. Webster*, Bud Hoey; *Chief Petty Officer*, Charles Martin; *Captain*, Frank Logan; *Radio Man*, Andy Jarrell; *Secretary*, Lora Kaye.

Black Eye. Warner Bros. *Producer*, Pat Rooney; *director*, Jack Arnold; *screenplay*, Mark Haggard, Jim Martin; *adapted from a novel by* Jeff Jacks; *photography*, Ralph Woolsey; *editor*, Gene Ruggiero; *sound*, Bud Alper, Gene Ashbrook, A. Gilmore; *music*, Mort Garson; *prod. mgr./asst. dir.*, Clark Paylow. *Running time:* 98 minutes. Technicolor. *Release:* April 1974. **Cast:** *Stone*, Fred Williamson; *Miss Francis*, Rosemary Forsyth; *Cynthia*, Teresa Graves; *Diane Davis*, Floy Dean; *Dole*, Richard Anderson; *Talbot*, Cyril Delevanti; *Bowen*, Richard X. Slattery; *Avery*, Larry Mann; *Majors*, Bret Morrison; *Amy*, Susan Arnold.

The Bunny Caper/Games Girls Play. General Film Corporation. An Arthur Marks Presentation. *Producer*, Peer J. Oppenheimer; *director*, Jack Arnold; *screenplay*, Peer J. Oppenheimer, James Brewer. *Running time:* 90 minutes. Color. *Release:* June 1974. **Cast:** Christina Hart, Jane Anthony, Drina Pavlovic, Jill Damas, Erin Geraghty, Gordon Sterne.

Boss Nigger. Dimension Pictures. *Producers*, Jack Arnold, Fred Williamson; *director*, Jack Arnold; *screenplay*, Fred Williamson; *photography*, Bob Caramico; *editor*, Gene Ruggiero; *music*, We Produce; *assistant director*, Nat Holt. *Running time:* 87 minutes. Todd-AO 35, color by DeLuxe. *Release:* January 1975. **Cast:** Fred Williamson, D'Urville Martin, R.G. Armstrong, William Smith, Don Red Barry, Carmen Hayworth, Barbara Leigh, Carmen Zapata, Bruce Gordon, Ben Zeller.

The Swiss Conspiracy. Bavaria/Durham (West German–American co-production). *Producers*, Dr. Helmut Jedele and Red Silverstein; *director*, Jack Arnold; *screenplay*, Michael Stanley; *director of photography*, W.P. Hassenstein; *art director*, Werner Achmann; *editor*, Murray Jordan. *Running time:* 80 minutes. Color. *European Release (Columbia-Warner):* May 1976. **Cast:** *David Christopher*,

David Janssen; *Denise*, Senta Berger; *Dwight McGowan*, John Ireland; *Robert Hayes*, John Saxon; *Franz Benninger*, Anton Differing; *Joe Korsak*, Arthur Brauss; *Andre Kosta*, Curt Lowens; *Tony Sando*, David Hess; *Hans Frey*, Inigo Gallo; *Corinne*, Sheila Ruskin; *As Guest Stars: Johann Hurtil*, Ray Milland; *Rita Jensen*, Elke Sommer.

Appendix I
Stop-Motion Dinosaur
Sequences and Matte
Paintings for *The Lost World*

These lists are here included to enable the reader to better visualize the director's intentions for the film and as examples of Arnold's meticulous preproduction planning. Page numbers refer to script pages.

Stop-Motion Dinosaur Sequences

Opening Seq. Shadow of Pterodactyl—P.O.V. Speck in Distance

Page	Description
45.	1. NIGHTFALL—SUNSET—Campfire PTERODACTYL flies in and grabs pig cooking over fire.
53.	2. DAY—On tree being used as bridge from pinnacle to plateau. Ed and Lucy attacked by PTERODACTYL. Shot at by Lord John. Pterodactyl dives under tree. (Pterodactyl flying at Ed and Lucy out of sun).
57.	3. DAY—(NEW SCENE TO BE ADDED)—Lucy wanders off making notes on Flora & Fauna—Long Shot into foreground a huge leg comes into shot. Then the body of a TYRANNOSAURUS REX comes into shot, looking at Lucy. Lucy completely unaware of the beast. She hears Challenger calling her, she leaves scene still unaware of the danger she was in.
58.	4. DAY—CAST follows two sets of tracks. Challenger, Summerlee, Lord John follow one set of tracks, Lucy and Ed follow the other tracks. Long shot—TWO IGUANODONS are feeding on a victim—on the right behind brush are Challenger, Summerlee, Lord John crouching, watching. Into foreground Ed and Lucy appear.

60.   5. DAY—PTERODACTYL ROOKERY—(See Script) A number of Pterodactyls—(See Storyboard).

64.   6. NIGHT—Lucy wanders away again from camp. Ed sees her empty blanket—hears her scream, picks up torch from fire and runs to her rescue. Thru thick brush the head and shoulders of a TYRANNO-SAURUS, mouth open, jaws dripping. Roars as if to attack Lucy. Ed runs in and shoves flaming torch into its mouth.

72.   7. NIGHT—PTERODACTYL ROOKERY—Volcanic Pit. Lord John lowers himself down into rookery amongst sleeping PTERO-DACTYLS. Finds dark volcanic fissure. Ignites a small torch drops it down, it vanishes from sight. He finds blue clay and digs around in it.

72.   8. NIGHT—INTERIOR FOREST—Ed moves thru forest looking for Lord John. He hears noise. He turns, looks up and stops in terror—he starts to back away. REVERSE SHOT. We see the huge and terrible shape and head of an ALLOSAURUS(?). Red eyes glowing fiercely and saber-tooth jaws dripping, wide open. With a fearful roar the great reptile lunges forward. Ed stumbles, drops his gun, he tries to grab it but the dinosaur is too close. Ed turns and runs for his life crashing thru the underbrush. Following shot of Ed running—the predator at his heels, BARELY VISIBLE we hear the sound of his crashing thru thick brush. Ed runs—suddenly falls into a dinosaur trap.

73.   9. INTERIOR TRAP—Huge skeleton head, empty eye sockets. For shock cut as Ed turns into it.

96.   10. NIGHT—ALBERT HALL—BABY PTERODACTYL out of crate—flies off over audience and gets out thru open window.

100.   11. NIGHT—EXT. BUCKINGHAM PALACE—PTERODACTYL flying fast, higher and higher over London ...... Into the darkness.

END CREDITS

Matte Paintings

Page 1   (1)   Matte shot that can be done at another location, somewhere later in the script on green set on the stage.

          (2)   Fast stream needed with wooded bank. Shots of the falls should be process. I have a plate from Africa that could be split onto a shot of river and canoe. Canoe over rapids area needs careful storyboard.

Page 2   (3)   Painting of 1912 London move in and dissolve to street and again to the window.

          (4)   Glady's [sic] parlor set.

Page 5   (5)   Matte shot of 1912 Fleet street (could be early evening not day).

            (6)   Editor's office.

Page 8   (7)   Same as (5) preceeded by staircase set, newspaper office.

Page 9   (8)   Challenger's house and street should be back lot. Needs short flight of steps and Victorian porch.

Page 10   (9)   Royal Society entrance (back of building semi-basement).

Page 11   (6)   Newspaper office could be part of Editor's office seen beyond his glass panelled door.

Page 12   (10)   Composite set of interior. Hallway and study no need for parlor as written.

Page 13   (10)   No need for stairs or two floors as written.

Page 19 & 20   Indian village and hut part of later location.

Page 23   (11)   Should be Queen's Hall not Albert. Need consider whether set or location. Interior should be set.

Page 29   (12)   Lord John's parlor study (should be Georgian as compared to Challenger's Victorian).

Page 30   (13)   To make this work it should be Grosvenor Terrace apartments or the like.

Page 31   (14)   Wharf should be researched around Ivory dock, London (MATTE).

Page 32   (14)   Could be same as 14 with Matte. Street (para) should be set.

Page 33   (15)   We need streamer and river so could make the L.S. matte with them rather than complete painting of steamer.

Page 36   (16)   Hotel front (Matte) and porch (Set).

Page 38   (15)   Village (minimal set) extended by matte.

Page 40   Cucuma village can be at same river location, narrowing river is matte, montage of mattes to progress up river.

Page 41 & 42
            (15)   All this sequence.

Page 43   (15)   Needs open skyline shots in here as well as wooded areas for
            (16)   this montage (typical second unit area with doubles to Wales or wherever).

Page 44   (17)   Studio set for night stuff (part of later scenes to be done for plateau sequences).

Page 45   (17)   If part of page 44 set it would need to be back-lot for long shots for flight of Pterodactyl. Climb up hill part of later location.

Page 46   Same as (1), need for location with base of cliff conformation (should look at quarry possibility) similar to Bronson Canyon (Hollywood).

Page 49   (1)   Cave exterior could be built onto (1) Interior should be set (half section).

Page 50   (1)   Suggest quarry because it would suffice for up shots and down shots. If there was need of location in Coales a remote slate quarry would be perfect for all the cliff and pinnacle sequences and the rookery.

Page 56   (18)   Studio set supplemented with mattes (back-lot).

Page 58   (19)   Wales again (Forest of Dean is near So. Wales).

Page 59 & 60   Need plates for dinosaur sequence to tie into location work around sequence.

Page 60 & 61   Heavily into storyboard here for B.S. and look into New Foundland cormorant footage.

Page 62   Campsite can tie into any of the convenient locations for lead into the back-lot set.

Page 66   Montage same location as (16). Fern meadow does not have to be as written, ferns essentially grow in forests.

Page 68   This calls for woods of very old trees with great gioths (there are some in grounds of Petworth House), Matte shots here too.

Page 71   Same as (17).

Page 73   (20)   Set and matte shots (on stage). Top of trap can be part of same.

Page 77   Edge of plateau can be one of the locations as it will be told with mattes but quarry is most likely.

Page 82   Indian village preferably back-lot with lake. Ape man battle should be close into studio for economy, it will include mosaics and mattes so need not be open country.

Page 89   (21)   The funeral on lake may necessitate location. Fires in London area prohibited.

Page 90   Quarry indicated again here. Base of plateau same as page 49
           or (l). Steamer deck on back-lot (22).

Page 90–97 Exterior scenes same crowd and set as (11) but matte of Albert
           Hall interior should be same as (11) but large set for Albert
           Hall in big studio for L.S. (23).

Page 98   Same as (12) perhaps it needs another set (24) different from
           parlor study.

           All told 24 sets and location sites. Location sites could be
           reduced if adjacent ones are found.

           Roughly 18 sets and 6 or 8 locations.

Appendix II
Screenplay Outline for
A Circle of Wheels

This outline for the screenplay of Arnold's most important unrealized personal film is here included to provide a clearer idea of this most unusual project than was possible in the text.

A Circle of Wheels
Outline for a Screenplay
by
Arthur A. Ross

Raymond Shaw was a brilliant student, Phi Beta Kappa, graduated first in his class at M.I.T. He was full of idealism and how he would help the world to be put right. He had his Masters as an electronic engineer, because that was where he knew the future lies.

What at the time seemed a tremendous bonus, the large multinational conglomerates vied for the top graduates. Raymond soon became a junior executive with the prodigious subsidiary of one of the world's largest conglomerates — Murchin Electronics, Inc.

Slowly and imperceptibly his idealism became the victim of conformity, office politics, climbing the rungs of the executive ladder, playing the game, living a little beyond his means, a bigger house, joining the "right" club, being with and associating with the "right" people. His dream a forgotten memory of his youth.

We pick up Raymond Shaw in his middle thirties, tennis playing, former electronic engineer who has become the Quality Control Engineer for Murchin Electronics, Inc. What he knows is that he is a junior vice-president of his division. . . . *What he doesn't know — is that he has a wheel — a small spoked gear — a cog, growing inside him.* He also doesn't know that his lovely, trim, one child, modern housekeeper, bright, efficient, sexy wife, Elsie Shaw, *too has a wheel growing insider her.* But she doesn't know it yet.

Charlie McReady is a management and distribution executive — equal to

226

Raymond in prestige, but not in knowledge. McReady's wife, Rose, childless, savage in her own way—is a sexy teaser who does it to provoke her husband—and destroy him, if she can.

The action often takes place at a "husband-and-wife" Saturday night poker game that is played from time to time at the Shaw's. Here Raymond heard the sound a little louder. So did Elsie. Four times they answered the doorbell that hadn't even rung. Twice Raymond short-circuited the remote control to the TV set but putting it too close to his *wheel in the liver*—although he didn't know he had one at the time.

Rose leaves the chattering poker group and follows Raymond into the kitchen and continues her game of: ". . . you're great, Raymond Shaw, you scare the hell out of my husband. . . ." Raymond denies it, always cautious. But she isn't: ". . . I'd throw up on Charlie, but then I'd have to take his suit to the cleaners and I'll be damned if I'll do anything extra for that fink. . . ." Rose, her weapons clear, moves to kiss Raymond. He asks if she hears a noise—a buzzing sound. Rose is puzzled. "Put your ear to my ear," Raymond says. Rose comments on his odd love-making habits—shrugs baffled. "Or was that the doorbell?" Raymond compounds the enigma.

Next evening, Raymond tells Elsie—after he has obtained the first results from their annual physical checkup: "I didn't even know we had a wheel in our liver!" "A *wheel* in our *liver*???" Elsie rises, screaming. "That's what the doctor said." Reasoning it out—they angrily decide the doctor's x-ray machine is broken. They go to the doctor and have confirmed that each had a cog, a wheel, in each of their bodies when the M.D. first took the x-rays, and there is nothing wrong with the machine. The doctor shows them the *new* x-rays, as he says: ". . . the two wheels . . ."

Raymond interrupts, impatiently: "I know, *she* has one and *I* have one." "No, no," the doctor says, barely keeping his medical detachment, "You now *each* have *two* wheels—*each of you*. You seem to have grown a wheel since you were here this afternoon. You seem to be growing a new one every six hours." "Nobody grows wheels!" "Except you and your wife . . . take two aspirins, drink a lot of water . . ."

In the Murchin Electronics plant, Raymond tries to go about his duties wearing the white coat, pants and cap to keep static electricity from affecting the delicately-calibrated electronic components being worked on for some anti-aircraft missiles. But one instrument inexplicably alters as he passes it—just a fraction. Raymond realizes he is the cause. He rushes out—with some excuse—leaves the plant and goes home.

At home—Raymond tells Elsie, his wife, he is becoming *magnetic*—just slightly—but his magnetism is throwing off units at the plant. Quitting is impossible. It would prejudice his being hired in any plant doing government work. If he tells—they might put him in an institution. He will have to keep grounding himself all day long, to make sure he draws off the static electricity. Elsie must do the same. And then he tries to rationalize his position—maybe this is the way it is supposed to be—". . . man to machine to *immortality*." As a scientist, Raymond revels at first in the idea of being a machine. He thinks he sees the end of the bicarbonate-and-aspirin era. It's wonderful to be a machine!

To be sure, Raymond goes to see Dr. Mark, Raymond's one time mentor and former professor, who listens as Raymond obliquely tries to justify the glorious triumph of machine-over-man. He tells him he feels like he is turning into a machine. (He doesn't dare tell him he means that literally!) Dr. Mark is sadly philosophical about what happens to most of his brilliant students who get caught up in the machine of conformity—and lose their most precious possession—their ideals. He tells Raymond he could always come back to academia . . . a professorship . . . replenish himself, in fact he urges him to do just that. Raymond goes back to the plant full of doubt and despair.

Back at the Murchin plant—chaos! Murchin devices have been found faulty! Military Intelligence suspects industrial spying and sabotage! Raymond's flawless record makes him eligible for counter-intelligence—to see who and by whom the instruments have been sabatoged. Seemingly Raymond is not suspected. But then the same Military Intelligence unit assigned Charlie McReady to watch Raymond. (Counter-counter-intelligence.)

Raymond just barely makes his case—clearing himself of personal liability and protecting himself—when he goes to the washroom—and sees an electronic component sticking to his back. He grabs a faucet; the component falls off. He has more and more static electricity and is becoming magnetic!

Raymond rushes home. Elsie is crying. All the electrical fuse-trip-switches in the house tripped out on the panel board. Raymond tells Elsie she forgot to ground herself. She does so. That night—baffled by the military intelligence units closing in, the wheels growing, they desperately search for the cause. Like an inventory, they tick off the orderly respectability of their lives. ". . . Sunday with relatives . . . Monday sit in with bills and checks . . . Tuesday, cabinet work in the garage . . . charities . . . or perhaps playing poker on Saturday nights . . . perhaps that was the sin—gambling . . ."

"Or maybe Charlie McReady has them, too? . . . but then if I call him and ask: 'Charlie, I have a terrible problem,' and he asks me what it is—what do I say? What *can* I say? And if he does have them—do you think that sneaky, lying informer spy would tell me?" (Beat.) "My God—I'm a spy, too!" Then a demand that both be honest. More honest that they've ever been with each other before. Affairs and all that. Indignation from Elsie—but then she has a startled awareness of something vital. "Our affair before we were married and I was pregnant and lost it!" Raymond protests—she never went for a test—it was supposition on her part. Besides, they got married. "But that's the punishment. We *never* paid a price for it. We are *now!*" Elsie says triumphantly.

Elsie is so relieved, but Raymond is more frightened than ever. "I want you, Elsie . . . I need you . . ." arms entwined—Elsie doesn't back away—but her words tell him: "Stop, Raymond . . . no . . ." *He releases her arms—but they still stand close together. They can't get apart!* "We're stuck—we can't get apart—we seem to have set up some kind of magnetic field between us. We have to ground ourselves." Then they lock step their way to the water faucet in the kitchen—where their son has come to get a drink of water. Very difficult to explain. They send him off to bed.

Still Raymond seeks his wife in pleasures they knew but she is too gratified with her discovery of the cause of their turning into wheels. "I'm so tired . . . and we're so magnetic . . ." Raymond angrily stalks off to the living room but he is followed by the worst of wifely kindnesses . . . "Well don't be angry, Raymond. If *you* want to—*I* don't mind." Raymond tries to turn out the lamp—his hand sticks to the chain. He grounds himself. At that moment—a high pitched whine is heard that scares the hell out of them—and the doorbell rings. It is Military Intelligence. The problem is worse than they thought. A component was stolen from the top secret room and found stuck in a toilet bowl. (Where it fell from Raymond's back.)

It is only a matter of time, Raymond realizes. Back to the doctor. Sixteen — (16) — count them — wheels in Raymond and Elsie. The femur and others are now forming into cogs, the doctor says.

Back to the plant. Raymond, while fulfilling his job — must avoid contact with anything electronic. He carries a chain which he drags behind him surreptitiously to draw off the static electricity. He is gaining a reputation for being a little bit mad — all within the past forty-eight hours.

Raymond gets into a violent battle with Elsie. They accidently touch — and are flung *away* from each other! They are now polarized in their magnetism. It spins them around. They *repel each other like dancing dolls if they get too close!* Raymond wildly, desperately, goes out into the night to find an answer.

Raymond realizes Charlie is trailing him. Raymond eludes Charlie — and goes to Rose, Charlie's wife. He knows Charlie won't be around because McReady is out, looking for Raymond. He won't really admit to himself what he's there for — but it is clear very soon. Perhaps an affair will be the answer to saving his life. Rose asks him why he is so agitated. Raymond begins: "What would you think of someone who was growing wheels inside him?" Responds Rose: "That is the most oblique approach any man has ever made to any woman . . ." But when the moment for real action begins, Rose evades. Raymond's realization: Rose is just trapped by her life as he, Raymond, is by his. She is trapped by hate for Charlie only because it's what keeps her going, but having an affair or hating Charlie won't save her life. "You'd better have a physical checkup, Rose." Raymond tells her, and he calls Mr. Murchin, further terrifying Rose, who sees Charlie's job possibly being ruined.

But telling Mr. Murchin why he came to see him is no easy task for Raymond. "I need more money . . . a bigger house . . . join the country club . . ." "You came here at four in the morning to tell me you need money for a bigger house and to join a country club? You'd better tell me the real cause . . . your job depends on it." "I'm growing wheels, do you believe me?" Raymond blurts out, all in one breath. Murchin — after a long pause — casually calls upstairs to his wife: "You'd better go to bed, dear! This is going to take longer than I thought!"

Coldly, precisely, Murchin says he has heard of wheels, but he does not believe in wheels; Raymond must forget wheels and work hard and not fight the establishment. In time — all rewards come — in time — not sooner and not later — but when he, Murchin decides. "I'll die!" Raymond shouts. "You won't die!" Murchin says. "After a while you won't even hear the sounds — there are no wheels. Forget them. Learn as I learned. It isn't of my making. It was made for me that way, too. Forget the wheels — or get out!" Obviously Mr. Murchin doesn't have an ulcer at all — he has cogs and wheels and rachets inside him — and he cannot even cry anymore.

Back home — there is no choice for Elsie and Raymond. *Suicide.* But they *can't* throw themselves into the river — *no sitter to leave with the child.* They can't kill themselves with sleeping pills — Elsie forgot to refill the prescription. They can't use gas. *It might kill their son, Albert, too. They can't hang themselves because they don't have any clothesline, nor have they had since they bought the electric clothes dryer.*

And all during this — the typical husband and wife battle begins — but mounts in fury. It reaches its climax of accusations from each to the other that doing things for each other was not enough; duty is not marriage; duty is not love; obligation is not love or marriage; that measuring what each gives is the disaster. All this is during the time Raymond holds three balls of heavy twine on a stick, *while Elsie braids a rope so that they can hang themselves.* But insight comes first—they see what they have been doing to themselves, the games they have played, the conformity, the values they have lost—*and somehow, unaware—the magnetic force is gone!*

Charlie McReady comes storming in and accuses Raymond of: (1) trying to rape his wife . . . his lonely wife; (2) being a spy; (3) trying to get Rose McReady to join him in some secret organization that had to do with big wheels, and (4) wait until Mr. Murchin hears all this!

Raymond blasts back at Charlie for the first time and says: "If Mr. Murchin *needs* me—he'll *keep* me. If he *doesn't*—he *won't.* I've been afraid you'd try to do something to me you've been doing all along. For me and Murchin, it's a two-way street. It works both ways, or it doesn't work at all!"

"What the hell is that noise!" Charlie demands. And he rushes about, trying to locate the whirring sound *only he* can hear—but Elsie and Raymond *cannot. They are free! They have been liberated.* Charlie, frightened, goes bellowing off into the night.

The next morning at the plant—Charlie McReady surreptitiously grounds himself with a chain. Raymond nods wisely, goes off, whistling, down the hallway.

Notes

Introduction.

1. Stuart M. Kaminsky, *American Film Genres: Approaches to a Critical Theory of Popular Film* (New York: Dell, 1977), p. 264.

Chapter 1. *Getting Started, or From Stage to Screen.*

1. A letter from Robert Flaherty to Local Board 251 of Elmhurst, Queens, N.Y., dated Sept. 18, 1942, reads as follows:

Dear Sirs:
   This is to certify that Mr. Jack Arnold is a Civil Service Cameraman assigned to War Dept. project S.S. #1 007 engaged in the making of motion pictures for the Office of Special Service of the War Dept. His replacement at this time would entail delay of the schedule that project is working on, and I feel that a deferment to the extent of fulfilling his present orders would be entirely in line with the war effort.

> Sincerely,
> Robert Flaherty
> Director, Office of Special Service
> War Dept., Wash., D.C.

2. *New York Times,* June 11, 1950.
3. *Ibid.*
4. *New York Times,* June 16, 1950.
5. *Motion Picture Herald,* July 1, 1950.
6. *Hollywood Citizen-News,* May 21, 1950.
7. *Los Angeles Examiner,* May 21, 1950.
8. *Hollywood Reporter,* January 14, 1953.
9. *Motion Picture Herald,* January 17, 1953.

Chapter 2. *Jack Arnold Explores the Third Dimension.*

1. Bill Warren, *Keep Watching the Skies! American Science Fiction Movies of the Fifties, Vol. I: 1950–1957* (Jefferson, N.C., & London: McFarland, 1982), p. 128.

2. *Hollywood Citizen-News*, December 31, 1953.
3. *Hollywood Reporter*, October 13, 1953.
4. When Miss Hughes (in a tight sweater) was introduced to audiences in *It Came from Outer Space*, the *Variety* reviewer remarked that ". . . sticks and stones are not the only things that can be projected out into the auditorium."
5. Frank D. McConnell, "Song of Innocence: The Creature from the Black Lagoon," *Journal of Popular Film* (Vol. 2, no. 1: Winter 1973), pp. 18–27.
6. John Baxter, *Science Fiction in the Cinema* (London: Tantivy, 1970), p. 120.

Chapter 3. *Infinitesimal and Infinite.*

1. Warren, p. 52.
2. Baxter, p. 126.

Chapter 4. *Tales of a Contract Storyteller.*

1. *Hollywood Reporter*, November 4, 1955.
2. A fuller disclosure of Miss Corday's charms may be found in the October 1958 issue of *Playboy* magazine.
3. *Variety*, April 19, 1955.
4. *Hollywood Reporter*, April 19, 1955.
5. According to *Daily Variety* (Nov. 26, 1954), Howard Pine, producer of *The Man from Bitter Ridge*, was originally set to produce *Red Sundown*, which was subsequently assigned to Mr. Zugsmith.
6. *Red Sundown* was Millican's last film; he died soon after its completion.
7. *Hollywood Reporter*, April 9, 1956.
8. *Variety*, April 9, 1956.
9. *Hollywood Reporter*, April 9, 1956.
10. *Variety*, April 9, 1956.
11. *Variety*, February 26, 1957.
12. *New York Times*, January 30, 1958.
13. Lou Valentino, *The Films of Lana Turner* (Secaucus, N.J.: Citadel, 1976), p. 218.
14. Todd McCarthy and Charles Flynn, eds., *Kings of the Bs: Working Within the Hollywood System* (New York: Dutton, 1975), p. 418.
15. *New York Times*, January 23, 1958.
16. *Variety*, November 26, 1957.
17. *Hollywood Reporter*, November 26, 1957.
18. *Hollywood Reporter*, October 14, 1958.
19. *Variety*, October 14, 1958.
20. Ed Naha, *Horrors from Screen to Scream.* (New York: Avon, 1975), p. 209.
21. Lee O. Miller, *The Great Cowboy Stars of Movies and Television*, (New Rochelle, N.Y.: Arlington House, 1979), p. 331.

Chapter 5. Spaced Kids and Space Children.

1. McCarthy and Flynn, p. 417.
2. McCarthy and Flynn, pp. 233, 242.
3. *Los Angeles Free Press*, October 24–30, 1975.
4. *Ibid.*
5. This tune was released by Sun Records under the title of "The High School Confidential Song" as part of a merchandising tie-in with the film.
6. Curiously enough, this poem was written by Mel Welles, credited for "special material." Welles is an interesting character, best remembered for his appearances in Roger Corman's early films, especially as the flower shop owner in *The Little Shop of Horrors*.
7. *Los Angeles Free Press*, October 24–30, 1975.
8. *Los Angeles Times*, February 25, 1958.

Chapter 6. The Mouse That Roared.

1. This is amply borne out by the contemporary reviews, which acknowledge Sellers as a sort of "poor man's" Alec Guinness, and consider him to have marquee value only in the U.K. *Mouse That Roared* was Sellers' first starring role.
2. *New York Times*, October 27, 1959.

Chapter 7. Ups and Downs of a Working Director.

1. *Variety*, October 31, 1961.
2. Leonard Maltin, *The Great Movie Comedians: From Chaplin to Woody Allen* (New York: Crown, 1978), pp. 193–194.
3. *Ibid.*, p. 194.
4. *Hollywood Reporter*, August 18, 1964.
5. *Boxoffice*, July 22, 1974.
6. *New York Times*, February 27, 1975.
7. *Variety*, September 17, 1980.
8. *Boxoffice*, September 19, 1977.

Selected Bibliography

Barbour, Alan G. *The Wonderful World of B-Films*. Kew Gardens, N.Y.: Screen Facts Press, 1968.

Baxter John. *Science Fiction in the Cinema*. London: The Tantivy Press/New York: A.S. Barnes, 1970.

Brosnan, John. "Jack Arnold: SF Film Director Extraordinaire," *Science Fiction Monthly* 1, no. 11 (1974), pp. 2–4.

————. *The Horror People*. New York: St. Martin's Press, 1976.

Cross, Robin. *The Big Book of B Movies, or How Low Was My Budget*. New York: St. Martin's Press, 1981.

Jung, Fernand; Weil, Claudius; and Seesslen, Georg. *Der Horror-Film: Regisseure, Stars, Autoren, Spezialisten, Themen und Filme von A–Z*. Munich: Rolof und Seesslen, 1977.

Kaminsky, Stuart M. *American Film Genres: Approaches to a Critical Theory of Popular Film*. New York: Dell, 1977.

Kelly, Bill. "Jack Is Back!" *Cinefantastique* 4, no. 2 (1975), pp. 17–25.

Krohn, Bill. "John Landis Interviewe Jack Arnold: Deux Cineastes Chez Universal," *Cahiers du Cinema*, no. 337 (June 1982), pp. 50–59.

McCarthy, Todd, and Flynn, Charles, eds. *Kings of the Bs: Working Within the Hollywood System*. New York: E.P. Dutton, 1975.

Maltin, Leonard. *The Great Movie Comedians: From Chaplin to Woody Allen*. New York: Crown, 1978.

Matheson, Richard. *The Shrinking Man*. Greenwich, Conn.: Fawcett, 1956.

Miller, Lee O. *The Great Cowboy Stars of Movies and Television*. New Rochelle, N.Y.: Arlington House, 1979.

Morgan, Hal, and Symmes, Dan. *Amazing 3-D*. Boston: Little, Brown, 1982.

Naha, Ed. *Horrors from Screen to Scream*. New York: Avon, 1975.

Parish, James Robert, and Pitts, Michael R. *The Great Science Fiction Pictures*. Metuchen, N.J.: Scarecrow, 1977.

Pedelty, Donovan. "He Came from Outer Space," *Picturegoer* (7/18/53) pp. 8–9.

Rubin, Martin. "The Incredible Shrinking Man," *Film Comment* (July/August 1975), pp. 52–53.

Sabatier, Jean-Marie. *Les Classiques du Cinema Fantastique*. Paris: Balland, 1973.

Valentino, Lou. *The Films of Lana Turner*. Secaucus, N.J.: Citadel, 1976.

Warren, Bill. *Keep Watching the Skies! American Science Fiction Movies of the Fifties. Vol. I: 1950–1957*. Jefferson, N.C., and London: McFarland, 1982.

Index

Page numbers in **boldface** indicate an illustration.

237

D

C